ORTHO'S

Deck Plans

Plan Designer and Writer: Robert J. Beckstrom
Writer: Ken Burton, Jr.
Illustrators: John Teisberg, Shawn Wallace

Meredith₀ Books
Des Moines, Iowa

Ortho® Books
An imprint of Meredith® Books

Ortho's Deck Plans
Solaris Book Development Team
Publisher: Robert B. Loperena
Editorial Director: Christine Jordan
Managing Editor: Sally W. Smith
Acquisitions Editors: Robert J. Beckstrom,
    Michael D. Smith
Publisher's Assistant: Joni Christiansen
Graphics Coordinator: Sally J. French
Editorial Coordinator: Cass Dempsey
Copy Editor: Melinda Levine
Writer: Larry Hodgson

Meredith Book Development Team
Project Editor: Benjamin W. Allen
Art Director: Tom Wegner
Copy Chief: Catherine Hamrick
Copy and Production Editor: Terri Fredrickson
Contributing Copy Editor: Carl A. Hill III
Technical Proofreader: Raymond L. Kast
Contributing Proofreaders: Steve Hallam, Todd Keith
Electronic Production Coordinator: Paula Forest
Editorial and Design Assistants: Judy Bailey, Kaye Chabot,
    Treesa Landry, Karen Schirm, Kathleen Stevens
Production Director: Douglas M. Johnston
Production Manager: Pam Kvitne
Assistant Prepress Manager: Marjorie J. Schenkelberg

Additional Editorial Contributions
Editor: Jeff Day
Writer: Ken Burton, Jr.

**Additional Editorial Contributions from
    Art Rep Services**
Director: Chip Nadeau
Designer: Laura Rades
Illustrators: John Teisberg, Shawn Wallace

Meredith® Books
Editor in Chief: James D. Blume
Design Director: Matt Strelecki
Managing Editor: Gregory H. Kayko

Director, Sales & Marketing, Retail: Michael A. Peterson
Director, Sales & Marketing, Special Markets:
    Rita McMullen
Director, Sales & Marketing, Home & Garden Center
    Channel: Ray Wolf
Director, Operations: George A. Susral

Vice President, General Manager: Jamie L. Martin

Meredith Publishing Group
President, Publishing Group: Christopher M. Little
Vice President, Consumer Marketing & Development:
    Hal Oringer

Meredith Corporation
Chairman and Chief Executive Officer: William T. Kerr

Chairman of the Executive Committee: E.T. Meredith III

Photographers
Ernest Braun, 3M, 7T, 14
Richard Christman, 7B, 8
John Fulker, 10, 11
John Holtorf, cover, 1
Michael Landis, 3B, 6, 36
Fred Lyon, 3T, 4
David K Swanlund, 9

All of us at Ortho® Books are dedicated to providing you
with the information and ideas you need to enhance your
home and garden. We welcome your comments and
suggestions about this book. Write to us at:
Meredith Corporation
Ortho Books
1716 Locust St.
Des Moines, IA 50309–3023

Note to the Readers: Due to differing conditions, tools,
and individual skills, Meredith Corporation assumes no
responsibility for any damages, injuries suffered, or losses
incurred as a result of following the information published
in this book. Before beginning any project, review the
instructions carefully, and if any doubts or questions remain,
consult local experts or authorities. Because codes and
regulations vary greatly, you always should check with
authorities to ensure that your project complies with all
applicable local codes and regulations. Always read and
observe all of the safety precautions provided by
manufacturers of any tools, equipment, or supplies,
and follow all accepted safety procedures.

Ortho® is a trademark of Monsanto Company used
under license.

CHOOSING A DECK PLAN 4

DECK CONSTRUCTION 14

DECK PLANS 36

CHOOSING A DECK PLAN

The most challenging part of building your deck may be choosing a design that works—both for you and your yard. The following pages illustrate some principles that will help you discover a deck plan that will enhance your home. Use these principles as broad guidelines in deciding what kind of deck is right for you. Notice that the location of a deck and the amenities—benches, furniture, plants, and screens—contribute as much to the deck's impact as the design itself.

A good deck plan grows out of the existing conditions and does not feel like it is imposed on the site. Take advantage of all the unique features of your home and site, as well as family needs and aesthetic preferences. Survey the site carefully to know what you need to take advantage of and what you need to overcome.

As you look through this book, keep in mind that you may need to adapt a plan to meet your specific situation. To this end, we have included some guidelines on how to adapt and modify the decks beginning on page 12.

Note how the railings, stairs, decking patterns, and site all work together as this deck cascades down the hill away from the house. This design combines both function and aesthetics to create a wonderfully unified whole.

DESIGN GUIDELINES: PRIVACY, ENCLOSURE, AND SCALE

A deck doesn't have to put you on display. Don't forget the use of a living barrier to screen you from the neighbors. Here a standard entrance to a deck mimics a hallway and creates an intimate sitting spot solely because of the surrounding vegetation.

A deck should offer privacy and a sense of enclosure. Think of your deck as an outdoor room, an extension of your living space. While it may lack a ceiling and walls, a well-designed deck still provides a certain amount of seclusion and privacy without losing touch with the outside world. Existing fences, trees, house walls, and other visual barriers can all provide shelter for a new deck. If none exist, you may need to incorporate a new fence or a fast-growing natural screen into your plans.

Because distance creates privacy, a deck surrounded by a large expanse of lawn or other landscaping may not need tall screening, but it should have railings, low benches, plants, or other amenities to soften its edges and create a feeling of enclosure and place, as well as for safety.

In more confined locations, the height of the deck may become an issue. Because most fences are only six feet high, a deck 30 inches off the ground may suddenly put you "on stage" for neighbors and passersby. One solution to this problem is to use a multilevel deck that has some platforms low enough for privacy and others high enough for access to the house.

A deck's size should be appropriate for its intended uses and available space. As a general rule, decks should be at least as large as indoor rooms with the same function. A deck intended for dining should be at least dining-room size, and one for outdoor gatherings should be at least family-room size—allowing for the fact that most outdoor furniture is slightly larger than its indoor cousins.

If your deck will serve more than one purpose, as most decks do, try to plan distinct areas for each activity. They can be separated by a change in levels, segregated by the deck's shape (an L or T shape, for instance), or defined by amenities like planters or overhead trellises. Include additional space for circulation and traffic flow.

Your deck should be in proportion with the rest of your house and garden, neither overwhelmed nor dwarfed by them. Local code requirements, such as setback limits and lot-coverage restrictions, may also influence its size.

If surrounding vegetation doesn't give you the privacy you want, build a privacy screen. Here a privacy screen was made from redwood plywood and lathe to blend visually with the redwood used for the decking. The screen doubles as a windbreak.

Designed for outdoor dining and entertaining, this deck uses a tree planter to define and separate activity areas while maintaining a woodsy feeling.

DESIGN GUIDELINES: ACCESS AND COMFORT

A deck should be accessible and inviting. People won't use a deck that is hard to get to. If it is attached to the house, it should be accessible from your home's public spaces, such as the family or living room. Decks intended for dining should be close to the kitchen or dining room. Ideally, the deck should have two or three entrances from different rooms.

The doorway itself should be wide enough to encourage flow between the indoor and outdoor spaces. French doors, atrium doors, or sliding glass doors (with approved safety glass) add to a deck's appeal and to a sense of continuity between indoors and outdoors. If the deck is not at the same level as the floor of the house, provide a transitional platform so you can go through the doorway without having to immediately step down.

Likewise, the transition between deck and garden should also be inviting. Design specific entryways and plan the landscaping around them. Make steps wide and graceful and install lighting for nighttime access.

Wide doorways create an inviting transition between the house and deck, making the deck actually feel like part of the room. Glass and screen doors maintain this feeling even when they are closed. Plants and furniture groupings also create a feeling of transition between the spaces.

A deck should be comfortable and pleasant. A good deck is designed for comfort, taking advantage of a yard's individual microclimates. The prevailing winds, the path of the sun, patterns of shade, and pockets of chilly air are all factors to consider in designing your deck.

If you want your deck to be shaded during certain times of the day or in certain seasons, you may be able to take advantage of the shadows provided by the house or fences, or summer shade provided by deciduous trees.

Depending on the prevailing climate, you may want to shield your deck from unwelcomed winds or locate it where it captures pleasant breezes. You may find that a high deck gets too much wind, while a deck set in a basin traps chilly air at night. You can control these conditions to some extent by choosing your deck site carefully, and you can modify them further by designing shading structures and/or windscreens to temper weather conditions.

This deck, situated in a heavily wooded region, extends out into a clearing to capture the sunshine. Other areas of the deck are shaded, offering a choice of sun or shade to suit individual preferences.

DESIGN GUIDELINES: HARMONY AND UNITY

A deck should harmonize with its setting. As you design your deck, try to imagine yourself looking at the finished project from various places—in the yard, in the house, and on the deck itself. The finished deck should blend in with its surroundings and look as if it belongs. Start by choosing materials similar to those used to build your house, and consider a deck that matches the shape of the yard.

A well-designed deck also has a delightful and appealing quality, a special something that makes you want to walk onto it and stay awhile. This appeal comes from all elements working together to create a unified whole. It also depends on some feature or theme that ties all of the deck's elements together. It may be a fascia wrapped around the deck, a repetitive railing motif, or a continuous bench or planter. It should be a simple and basic element, one that reflects a feature in the house or nearby garden structures.

Good deck design includes a strong focal point. It could be an object on the deck, such as a piece of furniture, a sculpture, or a large plant. Or it could be a panoramic view from one side of the deck. The simpler the deck design, the more likely it is to have a strong focal point.

This deck's design deliberately plays down the deck itself in order to not distract from the vista beyond. The uncomplicated two tier design and the transparent panels of the railing present the fewest obstacles to enjoying the view.

The repetition of a decking pattern visually breaks up large continuous spaces, and it can help simplify construction in many cases.

HOW TO ADAPT A PLAN FROM THIS BOOK

STARTING POINTS

Whether you are looking through this book for ideas and inspiration to design your own deck, or you intend to use one of the plans with little or no alteration, you are more apt to find a deck just right for you if you know exactly what you are looking for. Use the design principles described in the first section to help you identify your goals and priorities.

After you have picked a plan, you may need to adapt it to fit your particular situation. The following list discusses most of the changes you would want to make. These general principles can be applied to any deck, even though they describe a deck that is attached to a house.

TO ENLARGE A DECK

If you want to expand the deck outward from the house, the easiest way is to lengthen the joists. You can safely extend them beyond the beam (this extension is called a cantilever) as long as the length of the cantilever section is no more than one-fifth the total span of the joist. If you need to extend the deck even farther, you can add a second beam or move the first beam out and make all the joists larger.

To expand the deck along the length of the house, simply lengthen the ledger and beam and add more joists. The longer beam will require an additional post or two, or you can enlarge the beam and increase the spacing between posts. In addition to the structural changes, you will also have to increase the number or length of decking boards and make any railings or benches proportionately longer.

TO MAKE A DECK SMALLER

To shorten a deck along its length, reduce the number of joists and use shorter decking boards. The beam and ledger must also be shortened accordingly. If you want the deck narrower, move the beam closer to the house and use shorter joists. You will also need fewer decking boards.

TO CHANGE A DECK'S SHAPE

The easiest changes involve variations on a basic rectangle. For instance, wrapping a deck around a corner of the house or adding an extension will change the deck from a rectangle to an L. Structurally, this change involves the same principles as enlarging a deck, except that you are lengthening some of the joists instead of all of them, adding a short beam under the new addition instead of under the entire deck.

Another approach to varying the basic rectangle is to think of an L, or a T, or a Z, as separate decks joined together. Design the main platform, following the plan you are using, then design the additional leg as a separate deck to be joined to it. You may also be able to use parts of two different plans.

TO CHANGE THE DECK'S HEIGHT

You can raise or lower a deck by changing the heights of its posts. If you are adapting a ground-level deck plan for higher floor levels, be aware than most codes specify a maximum deck height (usually 30 inches above the ground) allowed before a railing is required. If your proposed height requires posts longer than 5 feet, you should add diagonal cross-bracing.

If you are lowering a deck so it will be closer to the ground, you can change its structure so that the joists are nailed into the face of the beam, rather than sitting on top of it. You may need to excavate in order to maintain at least an 8-inch clearance between earth and wood. You should also use heart redwood or pressure-treated material for decks close to the ground to prevent rot and termite damage.

TO MAKE A SINGLE-LEVEL DECK MULTILEVEL

For a one-step change in level, design the main platform as in the existing plan. If the smaller platform is to be raised, run joists under it just as if the deck were all one level. However, instead of laying decking boards on the joists where the platform is to be raised, run another set of joists crosswise on top of the first ones. Their depth should be the same as the desired height of the step, usually 7 inches. With this method, the decking on the raised platform will run perpendicular to the main decking, making the change in level more obvious and less hazardous.

If the second level is lower than the main platform or separated by several steps, it is easiest to design it as a separate deck system and join it to the main platform. Footings will usually be in the same places, as if the deck were all one level, but posts under the secondary section of deck will be lower or higher than the main platform. Where the two decks meet, the same posts can support both levels; just attach a stringer to the sides of the posts for the lower deck, and place a beam on top of it. See plans 5, 7, 8, 9, and 10 for examples of multilevel decks.

TO CHANGE FOOTINGS

Some areas may require deeper or larger footings than those used in the plan you have selected. The structure of the deck can remain the same. All you have to do is redesign the footing and pier. For steep sites, local codes may require drilled footings, or that all the footings be connected by concrete grade beams. Consult your local building officials to see what is required.

You may need to change the number or location of footings, to minimize digging, to avoid utility lines, or to take advantage of existing footings from an old deck. Such changes generally require redesigning the structure of the deck to reflect new joist and beam spans. The charts on pages 20—23 can help you redesign such structural modifications.

TO VARY THE PATTERN OF DECKING BOARDS

The easiest variation is to use different size decking boards—for instance, 2 by 4s instead of 2 by 6s—or to alternate decking boards of different sizes. If you want to use smaller boards than those in the plan, make sure the boards will safely span the distance between joists.

In some cases you can also change the direction of the decking boards. For example, if the plan shows them running perpendicular to the joists, you can easily run them diagonally. The joists will have to be closer together—close enough that the diagonal measurement from joist to joist still will be within the acceptable span for your decking. If the plan shows diagonal decking boards, you can run them perpendicular to the original diagonal direction. You could also run them perpendicular to the joists—and increase the joist spacing to match the span tables. You cannot run the decking boards parallel to the joists without changing the entire structural system.

TO ALTER RAILINGS

You may need to change the height of a railing to comply with local codes. Simply change the height of each post accordingly, and add or delete rails or alter the spacing to make up the difference. Other simple changes include varying the location of openings. Make sure the new design has posts wherever railing terminates or changes direction. Then move other posts, if necessary, to maintain uniform spacing between all the posts. If you change the post spacing on one side of the deck, lay out the opposite side to match.

The easiest way to change the style of the railing is to keep the post arrangement called for by the plan and alter the size or configuration of the other railing members, such as cap rail, stringer, and spindles. Because almost all railing systems begin with posts that are spaced 3 to 6 feet apart, you can put these in place and then attach horizontal rails and stringers, which in turn hold up any vertical members between the posts. If you choose a railing design that has a different post arrangement from the one in the plan, you can bolt posts to the deck's band joist or a 2-by fascia.

TO CHANGE STEPS OR STAIRS

You'll almost certainly have to adapt any stairs between the deck and the ground to suit your own site. The most important consideration is to make sure that all steps in a flight of stairs are exactly the same height, and that riser and tread dimensions comply with local codes.

Steps between deck levels or between the house and the deck will probably be the same dimensions as those in the plan. However, you can vary the design by using different types of tread lumber, different sizes of boards, or different size overhangs. You can also add risers or kickboards, if they are not included in the plan, to produce a more finished look.

TO CHANGE TRIM DETAILS

There is no limit to the decorative touches—such as planters, fascia boards, and trim—that you can add to your deck. In most cases they require no structural changes. The only limitations are aesthetic—be sure that these details harmonize with the house and yard, that they are not excessive, that they do not call undue attention to themselves, and that they maintain proportions similar to those of the deck itself.

Care and precision at every stage from the ground up makes for a beautiful, long-lasting deck. Here, you can see careful finish work at the step where the decking changes direction. This subtle detail adds to the deck's visual appeal while making the step more visible and therefore safer.

DECK CONSTRUCTION

Building a deck involves many skills, from layout and design to framing and finish carpentry. With some patience and attention to detail, even a novice carpenter can build a fine-looking, sturdy deck.

The process can be divided into three phases: foundation, framing, and finish. The foundation is what ties the deck to the ground. Putting in a foundation is the real grunt work involved in a deck. There will be holes to dig and concrete to pour. But despite the large-scale nature of the job, putting in a foundation requires working to very precise measurements. A little time invested in getting the foundation right will pay off when you start framing.

Framing picks up where the foundation stops—posts, beams and joists all come together to give substance to your design. Framing often goes fairly quickly, but care is needed to keep everything plumb, square, and level.

Finish work comes last. Here is where to add the details that make your deck livable. Extra care is required, because most finish work will be visible when the deck is complete.

In this chapter, you'll find an overview of each of these three basic phases of construction and some tips about how to accomplish them.

LAYOUT

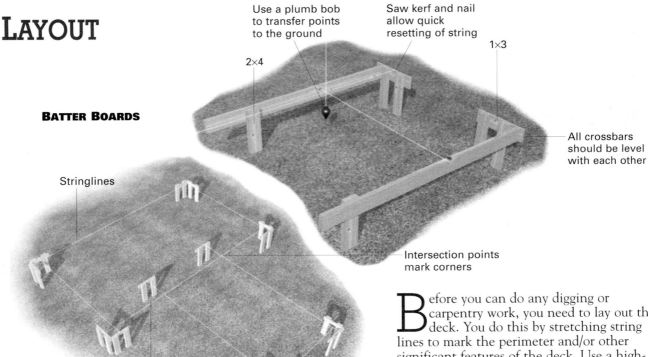

BATTER BOARDS

Use a plumb bob to transfer points to the ground

Saw kerf and nail allow quick resetting of string

1×3

2×4

All crossbars should be level with each other

Stringlines

Intersection points mark corners

Batter boards can be straight or L-shaped

ARE YOU ON THE LEVEL?

Once you start dealing with distances over about 6 or 8 feet, making things level to one another can be tricky. Most rental centers will rent you a transit or a builder's level that will make the job easier (and more expensive). Some use lasers to mark a point; others are small telescopes mounted on tripods. Either helps you pick a spot on a long pole that is level with the transit.

But there is also a lower-tech solution you can make yourself: a water level. At its simplest, a water level is just a length of clear vinyl tubing filled with water (no bubbles, please). If you leave both ends open to the air and hold the two ends along the objects you want to compare, the water in the tube will seek its level, allowing you to mark reference points on either item. You can purchase more sophisticated water levels that attach to a garden hose or which sound a tone when one end of the hose is level with the other.

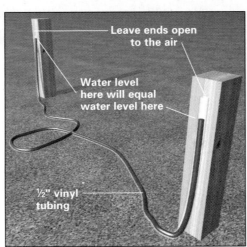

Leave ends open to the air

Water level here will equal water level here

½" vinyl tubing

Before you can do any digging or carpentry work, you need to lay out the deck. You do this by stretching string lines to mark the perimeter and/or other significant features of the deck. Use a high-quality string like mason's twine that won't stretch or sag.

For a deck that is attached to a house, you can use the house as a starting point. Attach the strings directly to the house and stretch them out from there. For freestanding decks, start by arbitrarily locating one side of the structure with a string and working from that.

The free ends of the strings are attached to batter boards. These small, fence-like assemblies are driven into the ground until their cross bars are level to one another—the strings must be level so you can make accurate measurements along them. Batter boards are usually set a few feet away from the actual corners so they won't be in the way when you excavate. The points where the strings cross each other mark the actual corners of the deck.

Once you have the strings stretched roughly where you want them, check to make sure they are square to one another using the 3-4-5 triangle. This method is based on a little high school geometry. Simply stated, if the diagonal between a point 3 feet from the corner on one line, and a point 4 feet from the corner on the other line equals five feet, the corner is square. (For more accuracy, use multiples of 3, 4, and 5 for your measurements.) If you need to make adjustments, slide one of the strings along batter boards until you get the proper diagonal.

When the strings are where you want them, mark their location by cutting a small notch with a hand saw. This keeps the strings from slipping and it will allow you to remove and replace them as needed.

FOUNDATIONS

The type of foundation you'll need for your deck depends on where you live. The two basic issues are how deep the ground freezes (if at all) and whether your area is seismically active. Consult with your local building officials to see what the local requirements are.

Local issues aside, most decks are built on top of either pier or post foundations. With a pier foundation, the deck posts rest on concrete column blocks which extend into the ground. The columns rest on larger concrete castings called footings which help distribute the deck's weight to the ground. With a post foundation, the supporting posts themselves extend into the ground.

To dig the holes for a pier foundation, stretch the layout strings and measure along them to locate the hole centers. Dig the holes down to the required depth below the frost line. If you have a number of holes to dig, consider renting a motorized post hole digger to make the work go faster. The diameter of the holes should be slightly more than that of the footings you intend to pour (usually 18 inches). You can nail together your own forms, but it is much easier to purchase cardboard tubes made especially for this purpose. Cut the tube to the length of the column, and screw a couple of 2×4s to it that are long enough to span the hole. When you put the tube in the hole, the bottom end should be 8-10 inches above the bottom of the hole. Level the tube and pour in concrete. The area below the tube will fill up with concrete, forming the footing; the tube itself becomes the column. Set adjustable metal post anchors in the wet concrete. They'll attach to the deck when the concrete hardens, and will still let you make minor adjustments, if necessary.

To build a post foundation, dig to the required depth, widen the bottom, and put the post directly in the hole. Be sure to use posts rated for "in ground applications." Brace and plumb the post so the bottom is roughly at frost line. Pour the concrete directly into the hole—it will form a footing in the wide bottom of the hole, and provide extra support for the post between the frost line and the surface. While these posts are sturdier in some situations, you can't adjust them once the concrete sets.

PIER AND POST FOUNDATIONS

Metal post anchor

Pier

Pressure-treated post rated for in-ground use

Grade

Frost line

4-6" of gravel-mix concrete

Rebar pin to link pier to footing

Footing (below frost line)

Undisturbed or well-compacted soil

PIER FOUNDATION

POST FOUNDATION

BASIC FRAMING

Even for the most complicated deck, the framing is generally pretty straightforward. Aside from the occasional miter, most of the joints are simple butt joints. Nails, bolts, and screws, combined with the appropriate metal hardware—like joist hangers and post anchors—will take care of most fastening. However, because most of the framing remains exposed to some degree, you'll want to take your time and be extra careful as you cut and assemble the pieces so they fit well and don't display hammer dings.

The drawings below give an overview of how most decks go together and what the various parts are called. This will vary somewhat, depending on what part of the country you live in. Also included in this section are four tables listing what size lumber is necessary for a given situation. Consult these charts as you begin to put your plan together to make sure your construction is strong enough to support the necessary loads. Keep in mind these figures are minimum standards. If your design calls for pieces that are near the maximum allowable span, consider going with the next size larger pieces. The slight cost increase will be well worth it.

BASIC RAILING COMPONENTS

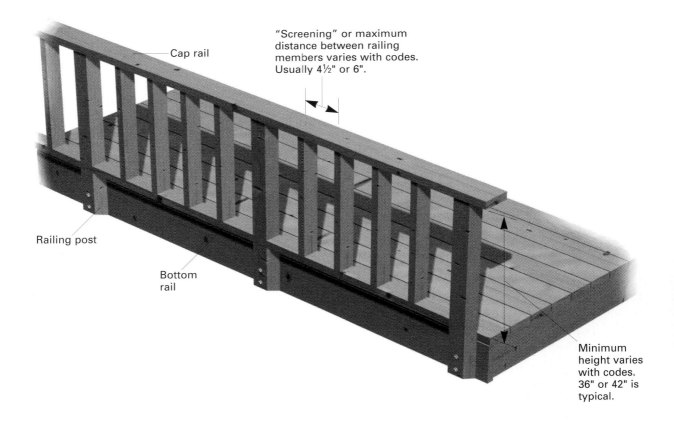

Cap rail

"Screening" or maximum distance between railing members varies with codes. Usually 4½" or 6".

Railing post

Bottom rail

Minimum height varies with codes. 36" or 42" is typical.

BASIC DECK COMPONENTS

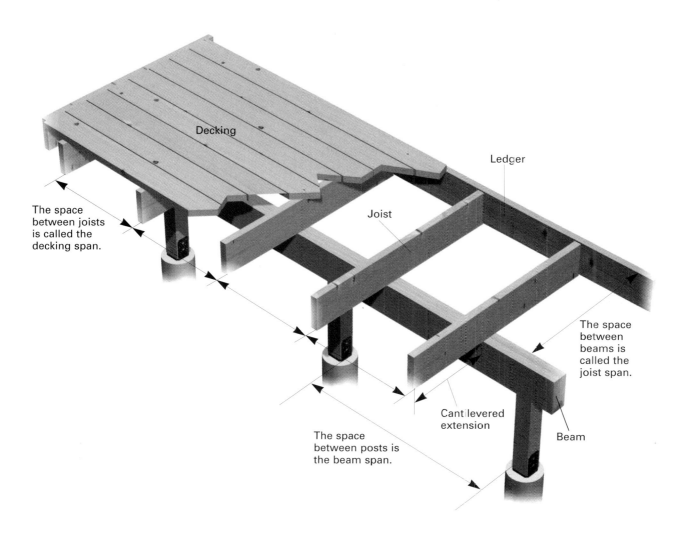

Decking

Ledger

Joist

The space between joists is called the decking span.

The space between beams is called the joist span.

Cantilevered extension

The space between posts is the beam span.

Beam

RECOMMENDED MAXIMUM SPANS FOR SPACED DECK BOARDS [1]

Species group	Maximum allowable span [2] (inches)					
	Laid flat				Laid on edge	
	1×6	2×3	2×4	2×6	2×3	2×4
1 Douglas fir, larch, and southern pine	24	28	32	48	84	96
2 Hem fir and Douglas fir south	16	24	28	42	72	84
3 Western pines and cedars, redwood, and spruces	16	24	24	36	60	72

[1] *These spans are based on the assumption that more than one floorboard carries normal loads. If concentrated loads are a rule, spans should be reduced accordingly.*

[2] *Based on construction grade or better (Select Structural, Appearance, no. 1 or no. 2).*

BASIC FRAMING
continued

JOIST SPANS (BEAM SPACING)[1]

Species group	Joist size (inches)	Joist spacing		
		16"	24"	32"
1 Douglas fir, larch, and	2×6	9'11"	7'11"	6'2"
southern pine	2×8	12'	10'6"	8'1"
	2×10	15'3"	13'4"	10'4"
2 Hem fir and Douglas fir south	2×6	8'7"	7'0"	5'8"
	2×8	11'4"	9'3"	7'6"
	2×10	14'6"	11'10"	9'6"
3 Western pines and cedars,	2×6	7'9"	6'2"	5'0"
redwood, and spruces	2×8	10'2"	8'1"	6'8"
	2×10	13'0"	10'4"	8'6"

[1] *Joists are on edge. Spans are center-to-center distances between beams or supports. (Spans based on 40 p.s.f. deck live load plus 10 p.s.f. dead load. Grade is no. 2 or better; no. 2 medium-grain southern pine.)*

CALCULATING SPANS

Determine the structure of your deck in exactly the opposite way that you actually build it. To do this, you start at the top and work down. Building starts at the bottom and goes up.

There are four basic parts of a deck's structure for which you need to determine the size: decking, joists, beams, and posts. Once you decide the type of decking to use and the size deck you want, you've set the stage for all other structural members below.

Before going further, find out what species of wood you'll be using because different woods have different properties which affect span lengths. For example, assume you're using western pine for an 8-foot-high, 10×18-foot deck with 1×6 decking boards laid flat. You would use the following steps to determine the structure to support it.

1. Start with **Recommended Maximum Spans for Spaced Deck Boards** on page 19, which shows that the joists need to be 16 inches apart on center.

2. The table **Joist Spans (Beam Spacing)** shows that 2×8 joists of western pine can span 10'2". This is the maximum allowable distance between beams. Because the deck is only 10 feet wide, two beams running along the edges of an 18-foot dimension would be 10 feet apart and therefore close enough together.

3. The table **Beam Spans (Post Spacing)** shows how far apart the posts under the beam should be. Because this example deck would have two beams roughly 10 feet apart and a 4×10 of western pine is desired, the posts would need to be no more than 6 feet apart.

4. Post size is determined by the "live load." A formula to calculate live load and an example are at the bottom of the chart **Minimum Post Sizes (Wood Beam Supports)**. Live load is determined by multiplying beam span by post spacing. It's easiest to estimate post spacing, calculate the live load, then adjust the post size or post spacing to build a secure deck.

BEAM SPANS (POST SPACING)[1]

Species group	Beam size (inches)	Beam spacing[2] (feet) (joist span)								
		4	5	6	7	8	9	10	11	12
1 Douglas fir, larch, and southern pine	4×6	Up to 6'——►								
	3×8	Up to 8'——►		Up to 7'	Up to6'——►					
	4×8	Up to 10'	Up to 9'	Up to 8'	Up to 7'——►		Up to 6'——►			
	3×10	Up to 11'	Up to 10'	Up to 9'	Up to 8'——►		Up to 7'——►		Up to 6'——►	
	4×10	Up to 12'	Up to 11'	Up to 10'	Up to 9'——►		Up to 8'——►		Up to 7'——►	
	3×12		Up to 12'	Up to 11'	Up to 10'	Up to 9'——►		Up to 8'——►		
	4×12			Up to 12'——►		Up to 11'	Up to 10'——►		Up to 9'——►	
	6×10					Up to 12'	Up to 11'	Up to 10'——►		
2 Hem fir and Douglas fir south	4×6	Up to 6'——►								
	3×8	Up to 7'——►		Up to6'——►						
	4×8	Up to 9'	Up to 8'	Up to 7'——►		Up to 6'				
	3×10	Up to 10'	Up to 9'	Up to 8'	Up to 7'——►		Up to6'——►			
	4×10	Up to 11'	Up to 10'	Up to 9'	Up to 8'——►		Up to 7'——►		Up to 6'	
	3×12	Up to 12'	Up to 11'	Up to 10'	Up to 9'	Up to 8'——►		Up to 7'——►		
	4×12		Up to 12'	Up to 11'	Up to 10'——►		Up to 9'——►		Up to 8'——►	
	6×10			Up to 12'	Up to 11'	Up to 10'——►		Up to 9'——►		
3 Western pines and cedars, redwood, and spruces	4×6	Up to 6'								
	3×8	Up to 7'	Up to 6'							
	4×8	Up to 8'	Up to 7'	Up to 6'——►						
	3×10	Up to 9'	Up to 8'	Up to 7'	Up to 6'——►					
	4×10	Up to 10'	Up to 9'	Up to 8'——►		Up to 7'——►		Up to 6'——►		
	3×12	Up to 11'	Up to 10'	Up to 9'	Up to 8'	Up to 7'——►			Up to 6'——►	
	4×12	Up to 12'	Up to 11'	Up to 10'	Up to 9'——►		Up to 8'——►		Up to 7'——►	
	6×10			Up to 12'	Up to 11'	Up to 10'	Up to 9'——►		Up to 8'——►	

[1] Beams are on edge. Spans are center-to-center distances between posts or supports. (Based on 40 p.s.f. deck live load plus 10 p.s.f. dead load. Grade is no. 2 or better; no. 2, medium-grain southern pine.)

[2] Example: If the beams are 9'8" apart and the species is Group 2, use the 10' column; 3x10 up to 6' spans, 4x10 up to 7', etc.

MINIMUM POST SIZES[1] (WOOD BEAM SUPPORTS)

Species group	Post size (inches)	Load area[2] : beam spacing x post spacing (square feet)									
		36	48	60	72	84	96	108	120	132	144
1 Douglas fir, larch, and southern pine	4×4	Up to 12'——►				Up to 10'		Up to 8'			
	4×6						Up to 12'——►		Up to 10'		
	6×6									Up to 12'	
2 Hem fir and Douglas fir south	4×4	Up to 12'		Up to 10'——►		Up to 8'——►					
	4×6			Up to 12'		Up to 10'——►					
	6×6					Up to 12'——►					
3 Western pines and cedars, redwood, and spruces	4×4	Up to 12'		Up to 10' ►	Up to 8' ►	Up to 6'——►					
	4×6			Up to 12' ►	Up to 10' ►	Up to 8'——►					
	6×6				Up to 12'——►						

[1] Based on 40 p.s.f. deck live load plus 10 p.s.f. dead load. Grade is Standard and Better for 4 by 4 inch posts and No. 1 and Better for larger sizes.

[2] Example: If the beam supports are spaced 8'6", on center and the posts are 11'6", then the load area is 98. Use next larger area 108.

DECKING

When it comes to adding the deck boards, details such as the species and grade of lumber, the board widths, and any edging all contribute to the overall look of your design. Consider each feature carefully; any one of them could dominate the entire look of the finished deck. Five factors will influence your choice of decking lumber: availability, durability, structural requirements, appearance, and cost. Start by finding out what durable species are readily available in your area and compare them to your budget. This may settle the issue immediately. If you have some choice, you can start thinking about the way you want your deck to look and how you're going to finish it.

CHOOSING THE LUMBER SPECIES GRADE

Many decks are left to weather naturally. So the appearance isn't so much based on what the wood looks like when it is new, but what it will look like after being exposed for a couple of seasons. Of the two most common naturally-durable species, cedar weathers to a fine, silvery gray, while redwood tends to darken. Most pressure-treated lumber tends to gray as well, but it can keep its green or brownish cast for quite a while. Another option is to use a man-made decking like Trex, which weathers quickly to either gray or brown, depending on the type you choose. If you intend to stain or paint the deck, your

DECKING PATTERNS

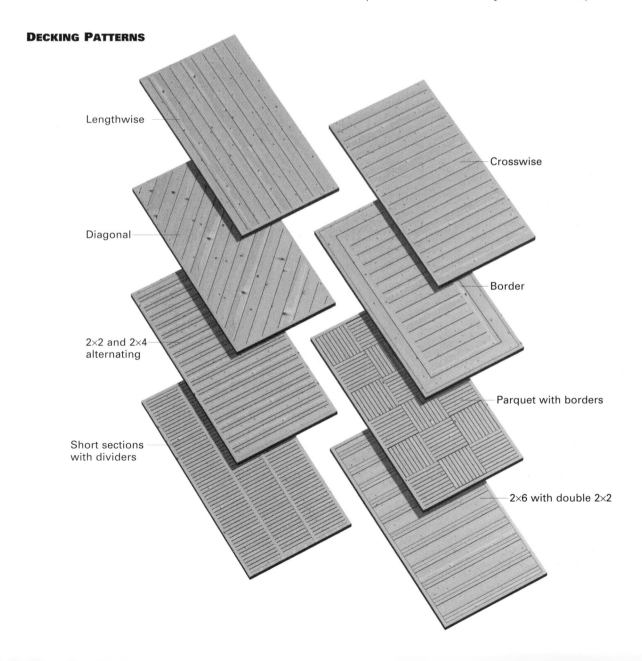

Lengthwise

Crosswise

Diagonal

Border

2×2 and 2×4 alternating

Parquet with borders

Short sections with dividers

2×6 with double 2×2

choice of wood will depend on its ability to hold stain or paint rather than on its color characteristics.

Knots and other defects are other factors to consider structurally, aesthetically, and as a safety issue. Better grades of lumber tend to have fewer knots, splits and other defects, but they are also more expensive. A good grade of lumber may be necessary if your design calls for the decking span to be close to the maximum allowed. It may also be a good idea in order to avoid splintering in areas where there will be a lot of barefoot traffic.

If necessary, you can get a mixed order of lumber with some premium boards and some with imperfections. Use the best boards at doorways, on steps and high-traffic areas, and along the edge of the deck.

CHOOSING THE SIZE OF LUMBER

Whether your boards should be 2×4s, 2×6s, 2×2s, or some other size depends on the pattern you select, as shown on the opposite page. There are also two other considerations that may affect your choice. Be sure the boards can safely span the distance between joists, especially in diagonal patterns. Also, it is best to avoid boards wider than 2×6 because they warp easily and drain poorly.

SELECTING A PATTERN

The possibilities for creating patterns out of decking boards are almost endless, but there are only a few that would be successful on any given deck. A few general principles, along with the illustrated examples, will help guide you in choosing a pattern.
■ On long rectangular decks, boards laid crosswise create a somewhat serene and restful feeling. Boards laid the long way accentuate the length of the deck and "drive" you from one end to the next rather than invite you to stay and rest.
■ Borders, whether a single-trim board or a wide margin, give a finished feeling to the deck.
■ On small decks, simple patterns work better than intricate patterns.
■ If boards are laid diagonally, it should be for a clear reason. They should reflect a dominant angle in the house or landscape, direct the eye to a clear focal point, or guide traffic to a doorway or stairs.
■ Complex or intricate patterns accentuate rather than hide the defects in boards. Therefore, use premium grade lumber for these projects. Otherwise, simply consider painting the boards.

CHOOSING FASTENERS

Nails are the least expensive option for fastening the deck boards to the frame. For the best appearance, you must be careful to maintain straight lines. Use only high-quality, corrosion-resistant nails, and take precautions to avoid splitting the board ends. Nails work well with decking boards that are crooked and need to be straightened as they are installed. On the down side, they can "pop"—come loose—from time to time, leaving an exposed hazard to barefoot navigation. They also puncture the top edge of the joists, which over time can lead to water penetration and splitting if the joists are not treated or painted first.

Galvanized deck screws are another option. While they are somewhat more expensive than nails, they will not pop. Use a heavy-duty power screw driver to sink the screws. If you'd like the look of a surface free of nails or screws, get deck clips that allow you to attach the boards by screwing into the side.

LOCATING END JOINTS

If the deck is longer than individual decking boards, the boards will have to be joined at several places. The illustration shows three options: one long, continuous joint; random joints; and intentional joint patterns. The main thing is to select your pattern beforehand and follow it consistently.

JOINT PATTERNS

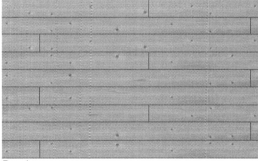
Continuous

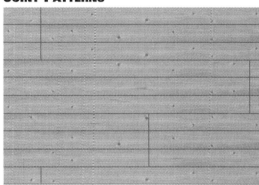
Random

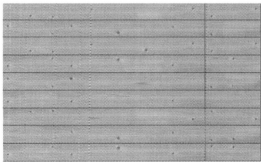
Pattern

RAILINGS

Railings are required on decks any time the deck elevation is greater than 30 inches—in some areas, railing may be required on decks that are lower. The building code will also dictate some of the railing's features, such as height (usually a minimum of 36 inches), maximum distance between railing members (often 4 inches), and lateral strength (15 pounds per lineal foot resistance). The rest of the design is up to you.

Plan your railing at the same time you design the rest of your deck—its design could influence the deck's basic structure, such as the location of posts. The railing will also have a strong impact on the deck's appearance.

Start by considering the character of your house and its trim. Is it formal, or more casual? Are its lines primarily horizontal or vertical? What kind of shapes are featured? Such questions will help you determine which railing designs may fit better than others. If you are not sure, stay with simple and basic designs.

Also consider the practical side. Is wind a factor? Will you want to set food and drinks on top of the railing? Is privacy needed? Get further direction by looking at pictures and actual railings for ideas that might work. By the time you have finished, the railing will almost have designed itself.

These four pages are intended to show the construction details for a variety of simple railing designs. In most cases, metal framing connectors or toenailing into predrilled holes will hold together any boards that can not be face-nailed or screwed.

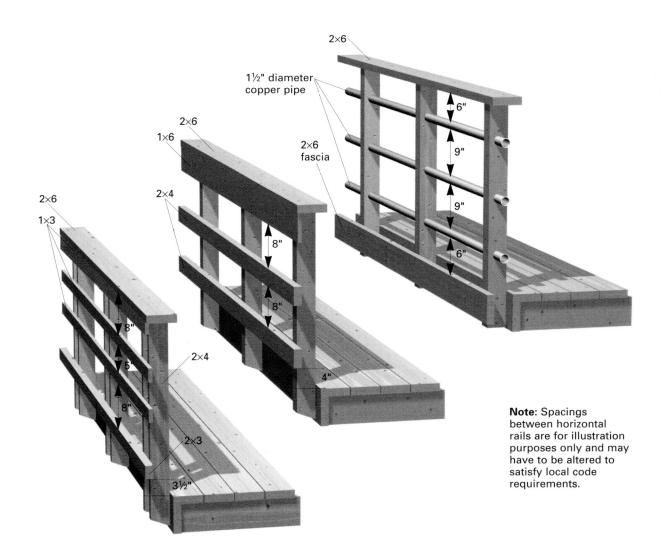

Note: Spacings between horizontal rails are for illustration purposes only and may have to be altered to satisfy local code requirements.

VERTICAL RAILINGS

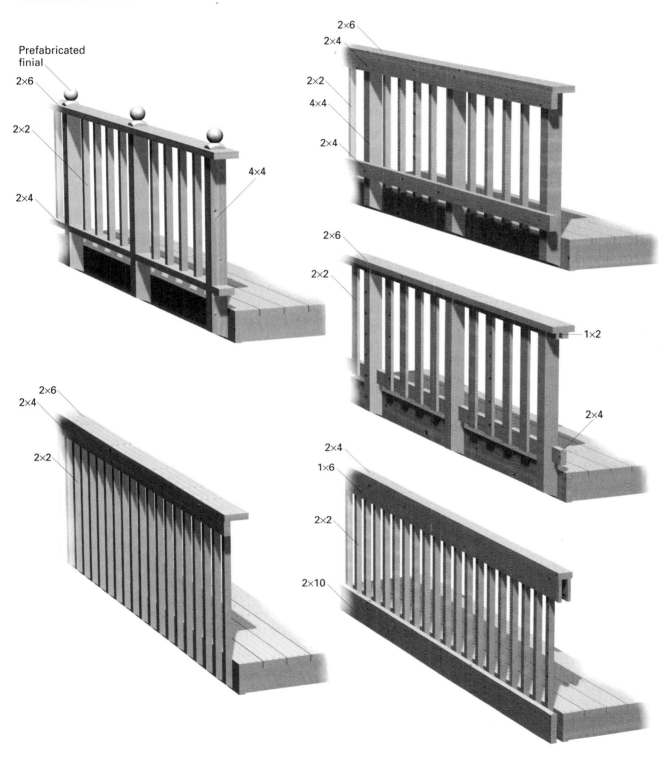

Prefabricated finial

2×6

2×2

2×4

4×4

2×6
2×4

2×2

4×4

2×4

2×6

2×2

1×2

2×4

2×6
2×4

2×2

2×4

1×6

2×2

2×10

RAILINGS
continued

RAILINGS WITH A VIEW

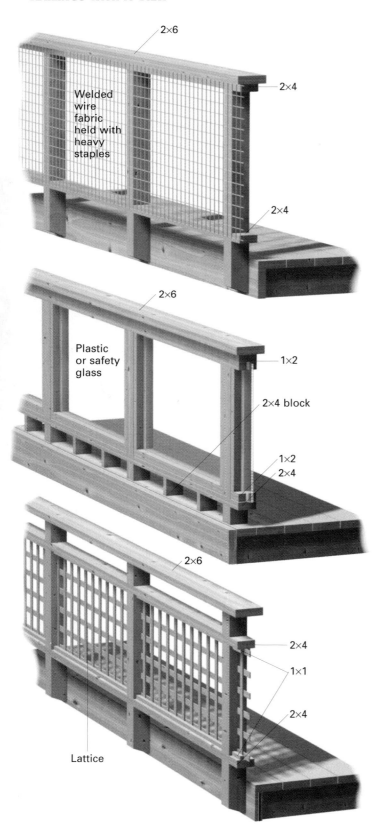

2×6

2×4

Welded
wire
fabric
held with
heavy
staples

2×4

2×6

Plastic
or safety
glass

1×2

2×4 block

1×2
2×4

2×6

2×4

1×1

2×4

Lattice

There are times when even a 36-inch-high railing might block a desirable view. In this situation, a see-through railing might be in order. One way to build a see-through rail is to fill the area between the posts with wire screening. This screening, called welded fabric, comes in rolls of various widths and with various mesh dimensions, such as 1"×2", 2"×1", and 3"×3". It is available galvanized or covered with colored vinyl. You can attach the wire to the posts and stringers with galvanized fencing staples. Align the wire carefully at the very beginning. A crooked start is impossible to straighten later on.

Glass or plastic panels are another option, especially if you also need a windbreak. Any glass must meet code requirements, which usually means safety or tempered glass. Plastics commonly used are acrylic (such as Plexiglas), which scratches and even splits fairly easily, and polycarbonate (like Lexan), which is very durable but also expensive. Both plastics expand and contract a great deal, so leave room around their edges. They also tend to discolor over time.

If some privacy is as important as visibility, the answer is a railing that is partially solid but has an opening below the cap rail. The example here uses lattice for the screening, but any solid fencing or siding material could be used.

SOLID RAILINGS

Solid railings are an excellent way to tie a new deck to the existing architecture, because they can be covered with the same siding material as the house. They also give the deck a very finished look.

The main problem is that solid railings are expensive because of the quantity of material required. They are also prone to moisture damage because they create an enclosed space were water can accumulate. The best way to prevent this problem is to provide a moisture barrier at the top of the railing and to use pressure-treated lumber for framing.

Put the moisture barrier at the top of the railing, under the cap rail, so water won't get inside the railing. You can use heavy building paper, like #30 felt, or metal flashing. As long as the siding material is applied carefully, it should waterproof the sides. The siding on the deck side of the railing should end slightly above the decking boards, allowing water to escape and air to circulate. The outside can either terminate at the same level or extend lower to become a screen.

PRIVACY SCREEN

For privacy, you may want to increase the height of a rail until it becomes a screen. Many materials could be used, including fencing, plants, fabric, or siding to match the house. This example shows plywood siding nailed to a simple stud wall that extends below the deck on the outside. Fencing materials also make excellent screens.

SOLID RAILINGS

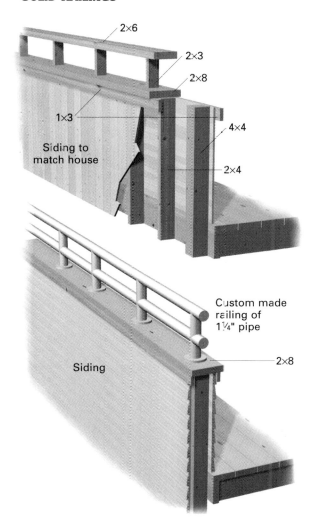

2×6
2×3
2×8
1×3
4×4
2×4
Siding to match house

Custom made railing of 1¼" pipe
Siding
2×8

PRIVACY SCREEN

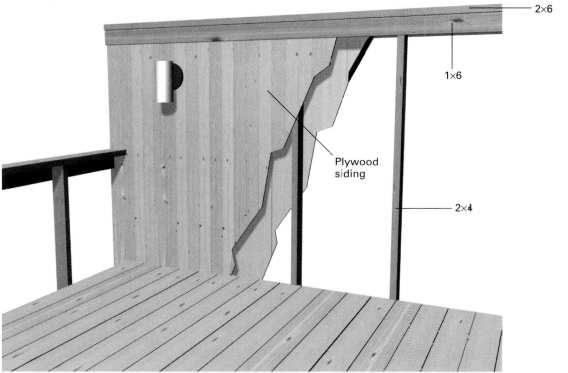

2×6
1×6
Plywood siding
2×4

STAIRS AND STEPS

You'll need stairs in a number of situations—for access to the house, changes in platform levels, or to connect separate decks. It is very important, for safety's sake, that all steps around the same deck level have the same rise and the same tread width.

If one or two steps are needed, the easiest way to build them is to construct small platforms using 2×6 or 2×8 joists. For steps to the ground, you can use a flat rock, pour a simple concrete step, or improvise wooden hanging steps similar to the one shown here.

If a staircase has more than two treads, it should be constructed using stringers, as explained on page 30. But even if you're building a simple stairway like the one below, you'll need to think about the proper proportion. **Comfortable Tread/Rise Ratios**, on the next page, shows you stairs with steps spaced to be both comfortable and safe. In order to see which one will work best for you, you need to do some measuring.

First, determine the overall run of the stair—the distance from the front of the staircase to the back, measured horizontally. Divide this by the number of steps you'd like

to find out the size of each tread, measured from front to back. Look at **Comfortable Tread/Rise Ratios** to see what the rise for each step should be.

To see if the tread size you've chosen will work, add the rises together. If the total is equal to the elevation of your deck, you're fine. If not, try adding or subtracting a stair and redoing the math.

If necessary, you can customize the stairs, as explained on page 30. From this point, you have two choices. The simplest is to leave the stringers uncut and attach the treads using wooden cleats or metal stair angles that have been spaced appropriately. The more common approach is to cut along the layout lines to create surfaces to nail treads to.

No matter which approach you take, before attaching the stringers to the deck, cut them off at the bottom by the thickness of one tread so all the rises will end up equal. (This may seem odd, but it works.)

Attach the tops of the stringers to the deck using joist hangers, a ledger board, or bolts if there are handy joist or beam ends. Nail the treads in place. Attach railings to stairs with more than three treads or to stairs that rise more than 30 inches above grade.

SIMPLE STEPS

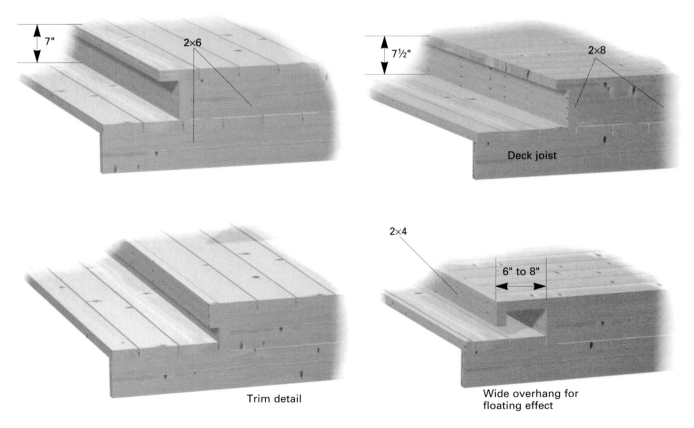

7" 2×6

7½" 2×8

Deck joist

Trim detail

2×4

6" to 8"

Wide overhang for floating effect

STAIR CONSTRUCTION

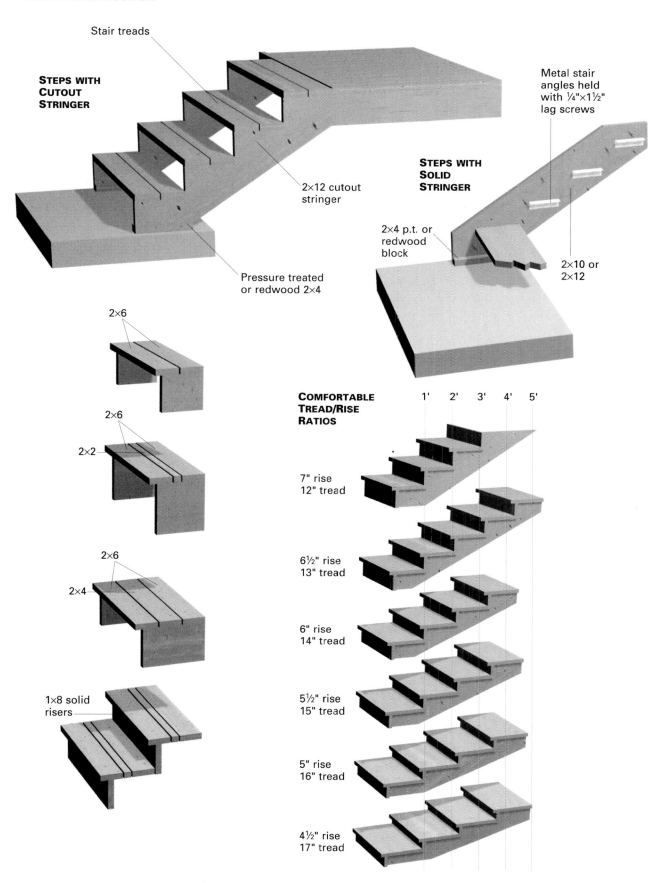

Stair treads

STEPS WITH CUTOUT STRINGER

2×12 cutout stringer

Pressure treated or redwood 2×4

Metal stair angles held with ¼"×1½" lag screws

STEPS WITH SOLID STRINGER

2×4 p.t. or redwood block

2×10 or 2×12

2×6

2×6

2×2

2×6

2×4

1×8 solid risers

COMFORTABLE TREAD/RISE RATIOS

1' 2' 3' 4' 5'

7" rise 12" tread

6½" rise 13" tread

6" rise 14" tread

5½" rise 15" tread

5" rise 16" tread

4½" rise 17" tread

STAIRS AND STEPS
continued

CUSTOMIZING STAIRS

No two sets of outdoor stairs are alike. Any of the stairways shown on page 29 may work on your deck. Chances are equally good, however, the treads and risers shown will result in a stairway that is too high, too low, too short or too long. If so, you will need to adjust the relationship between tread and riser.

The design of any stairway depends on two things: the height of the deck—called the rise of the stairway—and the length of the stairs—called the run. You'll need to know each before you begin building. The best way to measure rise and run is to drive a tall stake into the ground at what will be the foot of the steps, then plumb the stake and run a level line between it and the top of the deck. The length of the line is the run—the distance at the stake between the line and the ground is the rise.

The rest of the layout is a matter of juggling two rules of thumb: First, the ideal rise between two steps is 7 inches, although anything from 5 to 8 inches is acceptable. Second, for a comfortable climb and sure footing in rain or snow, the height of two steps plus the depth of a tread should be between 25 and 27 inches. Knowing that, you can begin to calculate the number of steps: If the total rise were 21 inches, for example, there would be three spaces (called risers) between the ground and the deck—each riser being the ideal height of 7 inches.

Knowing the number of risers, you can calculate the number and size of the treads. The number of steps is always one less than the number of risers, so in our example, there would be two steps. If the stairway length (run) were 26 inches, the depth of each tread, measured from front to back, would be 13 inches. The sum of two risers and a tread would be 27—within the allowable range of the 25 to 27 inches.

In the real world, it's usually more complicated. You often have to juggle numbers, round off, and maybe even adjust the size of stairway. Let's add a couple of inches to our example, making the rise 23 inches and the run 28 inches.

Dividing the rise—23 inches—by the ideal tread height of 7 leaves us with $3\frac{2}{7}$ risers. There's no such thing as $\frac{2}{7}$ of riser, so we'll make our first compromise—rounding the answer to the nearest whole number—3. If three risers total 23 inches, each must be $7\frac{2}{3}$ inches, or roughly $7\frac{11}{16}$ inches high, the number we'll use for tread height.

Three risers means two steps. With a 28-inch run, each step is 14 inches deep. So far, everything is working fine. Unfortunately the proportions of the steps are wrong: The height of two risers plus the depth of a tread is $29\frac{3}{8}$ inches—well outside the acceptable range of 25-27 inches. If you experiment, you'll discover the alternatives are worse: On a three-step stairway, the height of two risers plus a tread is way too short. On a one-step stairway, the total is way too long.

Your first option is to use the rise and run you calculated—three risers and two steps—even though it doesn't match the formula exactly. While not perfect, the stairs will certainly be navigable. If you've got a little bit of room to spare, however, you have a second option: adjusting the length of the stairway. Making the stairway a bit shorter or longer will usually force the numbers into line. For example, changing the run of our stairway to 23 inches would give you two treads, each $11\frac{1}{2}$ inches wide. The riser height stays at $7\frac{11}{16}$, and plugging the numbers in the formula gives us $26\frac{7}{8}$ inches—an answer within the allowable range. If moving the stairway uphill changes the overall rise of the deck, a bit of digging at the base of the steps will bring it back in line. If moving downhill increases the rise, you can correct it when you pour the base for the steps.

LAYING OUT STRINGERS: Once you know the general dimensions of a stairway, you can begin to lay it out. Traditionally, steps are supported by a sawtooth stringer, like the one shown in **Stair Construction, Steps with Cut out Stringer,** on page 29. The simpler **Making a Solid Stringer** are made with metal hangers sold at hardware stores and home centers. No matter which stringer you choose, the layout is the same.

Lay out the steps directly on the stringer with a framing square, as shown in **Laying Out the Top Step.** Mark the rise between steps on one arm of the square; mark the depth of the tread on the other arm. You can mark the square with pieces of tape, but the square will tend to slip around when you're trying to make marks against it. Carpenters avoid this by using inexpensive metal markers, called stair gauges, that clamp onto the square.

Place the square against the stringer at what will be the top of the steps, as shown.

LAYING OUT THE TOP STEP

Tape on framing square marks rise between steps

Tape on framing square marks tread depth

Stringer

Top end of stringer

Draw lines by guiding a pencil along each arm of the square. The long line marks the tread. The short line marks the rise from the tread to the deck. Extend the rise line all the way across the board to lay out the end of the stringer.

To lay out the next step, slide the square down the stringer, as shown in **Laying Out the Middle Steps**, and trace along it to lay out the rise and tread. Move down step by step until you've laid out the entire stringer. After you draw the rise that extends from the ground to the first step, draw a line that would mark the next tread, if there was one. The bottom of the stringer will be above this line by the thickness of one tread. Mark it by drawing a line, as shown in **Laying Out the Bottom of the Stringer.**

MAKING A SOLID STRINGER: What you do next depends on whether you want steps with a cutout stringer or steps with a solid stringer. For a solid stringer, lay out a second stringer as described above. Cut along the line marking the top of the stringer and along the line marking the bottom end. When you're done, draw a line parallel to each tread to lay out the bottom of the tread. Screw metal stair angles along the lines marking the bottom of each tread. Put the stringers in place against the deck, and screw the treads to the cleats, as shown in **Stair Construction,** page 29.

MAKING A CUTOUT STRINGER: Begin a cutout stringer by cutting out the top and bottom of a stringer, as you did for a solid stringer. Don't lay out a second stringer, and don't draw a line marking the bottom of each tread. Instead, cut carefully along the line marking the treads, stopping when the blade meets a line for a riser. Cut along the riser lines next, stopping when the blade meets the cut you made for the tread. Even though the cuts meet, the cut isn't quite as long on the underside of the board, so the waste stays in place. Finish the cut with a hand saw.

Once you've cut out the first stringer, use it as a pattern to lay out a second stringer. Cut the stringer the same way you cut the first. Put the stringers in place, and nail treads to the stringers.

ATTACHING THE STRINGERS: Metal connectors, available at most hardware stores and home centers, make attaching the upper end of the deck relatively simple. Without a solid base at the bottom of the stairs, however, the stairway will move slightly as people walk on it. Repeated movement will cause the stairs to break away from the deck—usually while someone is walking on it.

Sturdy stairs need to be anchored at the bottom. The best way to do this is to pour a concrete pad and then attach the stringers to it. The pad should be 30 inches from to back

and 12 inches wider than the stairs—6 inches on each side. Dig a hole 10 inches deep, and several inches wider and longer than the pad. Line the hole with 6 inches of gravel, and compact it by pounding it with a tamper. Build a form for a 4-inch pad, stake it in the gravel, and level it. Fill the form with premixed, bagged concrete, following the directions on the bag. Pull a 2×4 across the top of the form to level the concrete.

There are several ways to attach the stringers to the concrete. The easiest is shown in Stair Construction on page 29, where the stringer is nailed to a block that is attached to the concrete. This block can be nailed in place after the concrete dries, or can be attached to bolts set in the wet concrete. If you use either of these methods, trim the bottom of the stringer by an amount equal to the thickness of the block.

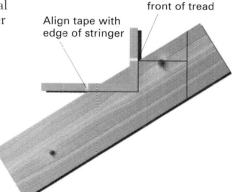

Align tape with front of tread

Align tape with edge of stringer

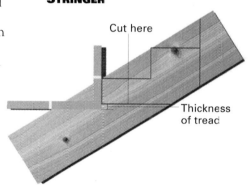

Cut here

Thickness of tread

DESIGN CONSIDERATIONS

Stairways are open to weather and get a great deal of abuse. Build them from a rot-resistant wood. Pressure-treated wood works well, but make sure you get stock rated for ground contact. In the West, supply keeps the price of redwood and cedar low, and they can be substituted for pressure treated wood, often at a savings. In the South, cypress is often used for the same reason.

Stairs should be at least 36 inches wide, allowing two people to use the stairs at the same time. If you make them wider than 36 inches, common sense (and most codes) say you'll need to add a stringer in the middle of the stairs.

BENCHES

Like railings, benches should be planned along with the rest of the deck. Here are a few guidelines to help as you develop your design.

BENCH CONSTRUCTION

To start with, benches should be from 15 to 18 inches high for comfortable seating. They can be built as an extension of the deck's framing or added after the deck is completed. For all of the designs presented in this book, the benches were built from standard sizes of lumber. This greatly simplifies construction.

No matter what kind of bench you decide to build, make the seats as smooth as possible. Round sharp edges with a router and then sand wherever necessary. There are also two methods for assembling seats so no nail heads show on the top surface. One is to toenail each slat from the side rather than face-nailing it down through the top. The other method is to construct the bench platform upside down, nailing the cleats to the slats from below.

BENCH CONSTRUCTION

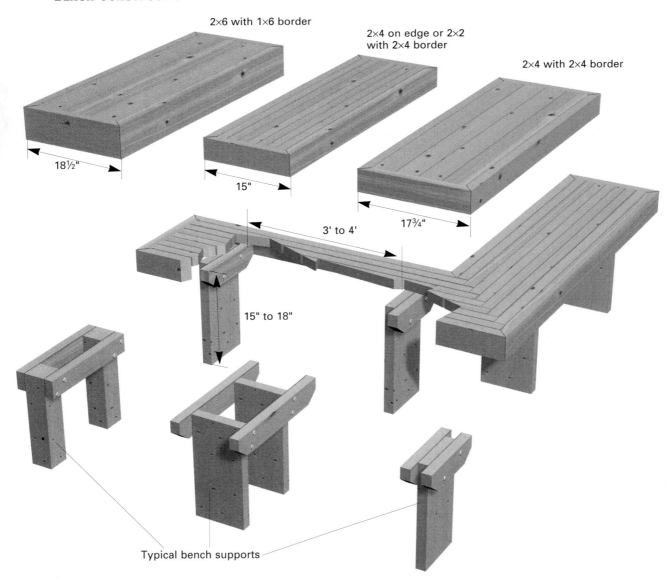

2×6 with 1×6 border

2×4 on edge or 2×2 with 2×4 border

2×4 with 2×4 border

18½"

15"

17¾"

3' to 4'

15" to 18"

Typical bench supports

ATTACHING THE BENCH

Benches that are essentially freestanding can be attached to a deck by toenailing their supports into the deck boards. To prevent splitting, the supports should be predrilled or secured to the decking with metal brackets.

There are also several ways to attach a bench's uprights to the deck framing or to incorporate a part of the deck's frame into a bench. One is to extend the deck's supporting posts through the decking boards. A second is to bolt uprights to the joists and lay the decking around the uprights during construction. A third is to attach the bench to the railing posts. This method is particularly appropriate for high decks where a 36-inch railing provides a back for the bench. It also meets code requirements. Note: In order to meet code a rail might have to be installed under the bench to reduce the size of the opening.

ATTACHING A BENCH TO A RAILING

ATTACHING UPRIGHTS TO JOIST

ATTACHING A FREESTANDING BENCH TO DECKING

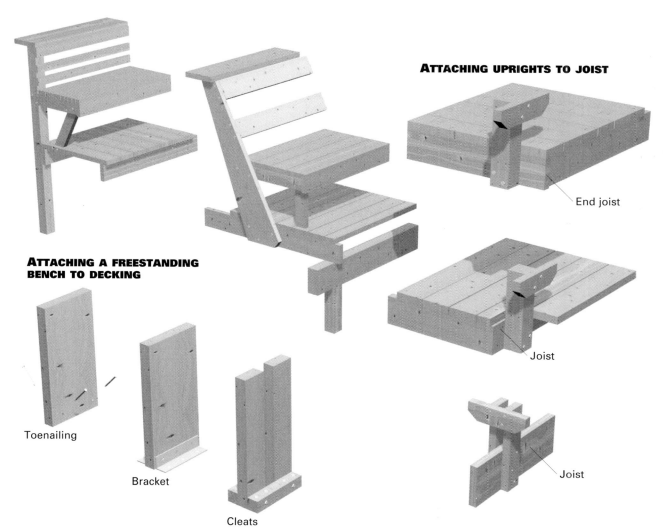

End joist

Joist

Joist

Toenailing

Bracket

Cleats

DECK FINISHES

Deck finishes, such as stains, sealers, paints, and bleaches, are coatings used to increase the wood's durability or to enhance the deck's final appearance. Some finishes do both.

There are many ways you can finish your deck, depending on the type of lumber, your preference of color, and the deck's environment. Here are some guidelines you can use in selecting a finish and applying it to various kinds of lumber. You may use the same finish throughout the deck, or you may choose to finish different parts in different ways. For example, you could paint the understructure and railings, but stain the decking boards or leave them natural.

It is important to realize that both your choice of finish and your choice of lumber play major roles in the deck's final look and its ability to withstand constant exposure to the elements, so consider these factors early in your planning.

Pressure-treated wood has become a popular material for deck building. Because the wood is pressure treated with a preservative, it's insect and rot proof even without the protection of a finish. As a result, many homeowners leave the wood unfinished and let it weather until it takes on a soft gray color. Pressure-treated lumber still comes from trees, however, and it will still crack, check, and warp, like any other wood. The damage usually isn't excessive, but if you'd like to keep the wood in top notch shape, apply a finish, even if the wood is pressure treated.

Most pressure-treated wood is kiln-dried before it's pressure treated, but not after. A great many boards are still soaked when they get to the lumberyard, and won't begin to take a finish. Others may be dry to the touch but still contain enough water to cause a finish to blister and peel. While you can build with any of this wood, you have to let it dry out before you apply a finish.

To see if your deck is ready for a finish, sprinkle some water on the wood. If the water soaks into the wood, the wood is dry enough to take a finish. If it beads and rolls off, put the paint can away, wait for a few weeks, and test again.

PRESERVATIVES AND SAFETY

An issue related closely to finishes is the health risk of handling certain toxic wood preservatives. The Environmental Protection Agency has banned a number of preservatives from over-the-counter sales and restricted their use to licensed applicators and manufacturers of pressure-treated lumber. The restricted list includes pentachlorophenols and inorganic arsenic compounds. Others may be added to the list.

The restricted preservatives are not available for use by homeowners, but you can still buy wood that has been pretreated with one of them. Avoid creosote-treated lumber altogether—the creosote rubs off and stains skin and clothes. Use any lumber that has been treated with pentachlorophenol for structural members only. Pressure-treated lumber is fine in almost all deck applications. Because it's injected with inorganic arsenic compounds, however, avoid it for any surface that will come in contact with food. Restrictions and recommendations regarding wood preservatives may change, so check with a competent retailer or local environmental authorities before making a final decision.

FINISH OPTIONS: THE NATURAL LOOK

WEATHERED WOOD: If you want your deck to have a gray, weathered look, the easiest "finish" is to do nothing. Just let it weather naturally. This technique works best with all-heart grades of a durable species such as cedar, cypress, or redwood. Pressure-treated lumber also weathers well, although the color is not strictly the same as the natural wood.

The final color and the length of the aging process vary with the type of lumber and its exposure, but generally cedar and cypress weather to a light, silver gray; redwood turns dark gray; and pressure-treated lumber turns gray with a hint of its original green or tan coloring.

NEW WOOD: A just-built deck of fresh, new wood has a beauty most people admire. The warm tones of the wood, its grain, its texture, and even its smell create a clean and appealing deck that seems to blend with almost any setting. Inevitably, however, the wood ages and the deck loses that same freshness.

Is there some way to capture that look of new wood permanently? Although there is no way to preserve the exact look, there are three treatments that approximate it.

One option is to prolong the look by applying a clear sealer. This protects the wood and slows down the weathering process by as much as a year, giving you more time to enjoy the wood's original color before having to do something else. Use a water-repellent sealer that penetrates the wood.

The second option is to apply no finish or sealer at all and let the wood weather naturally. You may then restore its surface periodically by scrubbing it with trisodium phosphate (TSP) and applying a special deck-renewing product. (Be sure to follow the manufacturer's safety precautions, including the use of rubber gloves.) After rinsing off the cleaner, you will have a deck instantly transformed from gray to original-looking wood. It will not have that smooth, clean surface of brand new wood, but it will have a rich, warm tone instead of weathered gray. Do not use this method unless the wood is resistant to decay, or it will not last long. To maintain the look, you need to repeat this treatment whenever the deck weathers to an objectionable color.

The third treatment is to stain the deck a color that matches the new wood as closely as possible. A semi-transparent stain will cover the wood with a colored coating, but the wood's grain and texture will still show clearly. Look for a stain that includes a water-repellent additive, or better yet, an approved preservative. Before applying the stain, wait for wood in the deck to dry out—usually 60 days. Use a semitransparent, light-bodied stain specified as a nonchalking or sealer type. It is best to do small samples first, in an out-of-the-way spot to make sure the stain is the color you desire.

FINISH OPTIONS: A CUSTOM COLOR

If the color of natural wood, either weathered or new, is not suitable for your deck, you can change it to almost any color imaginable by staining or painting it.

STAINING: Exterior stains penetrate the wood rather than coat it like paint, leaving the surface texture the same as natural wood, but a different color. Two types of stains are available: semi-transparent (light-bodied) and solid (full-bodied). The semi-transparent stains have less pigment than solid stains. They reveal the grain of the wood better, but they are not as durable, do not hide wood defects as well, and need to be renewed more often. Both have the advantage of retaining the soft texture and warmth of wood.

Most brands offer a fairly wide selection of colors, although the range is often limited to earth tones (browns, reds, greens, and grays).

It is difficult to predict the exact color of your deck because the same stain will produce a different color on different types of wood, and will even vary between sapwood and heart-wood of the same species.

Oil-based stains are more durable than water-based stains. The deck lumber must be thoroughly seasoned and dry before applying stain. Let a new deck stand for two months before staining. If you are staining the deck surface, use a light-bodied stain instead of a full-bodied one. The inevitable wear will not be as noticeable, and periodic re-staining will produce a more even color. Be sure you apply a nonchalking or sealer type of stain, so a powdery film does not get tracked into the house.

PAINTING: Painting a deck, or parts of it, creates an elegant, refined look. Unlike stain, paint completely masks the wood, making it an ideal finish for lower grades of lumber. Paint offers an unlimited choice of color, and it will not vary with the type of lumber used. Paint takes more time to apply, is more expensive, and is harder to maintain than other finishes, but it offers the best protection. Once you have painted a deck, however, it will be impossible to change to any of the other finish options.

For best results, the wood should be thoroughly seasoned before painting, usually 60 days. You can prime it beforehand, however, especially the ends and edges of structural members that get covered as the deck is built.

If you are painting the deck surface itself, choose a paint specified for outdoor decks or porches so it will withstand heavy wear. Like painted porches and steps, a painted deck surface can be slippery when wet. As an extra safety precaution, especially around doorways and stairs, you can mix a handful or so of clean sand with paint used for the final coat.

MAINTAINING YOUR DECK

In addition to applying a finish to your deck, you can prolong its life by cleaning and scrubbing it periodically. Use a bleach or other strong cleaner if the boards have any moss or fungus. Remove sand, gravel, and other debris as soon as possible.

DECK PLANS

This chapter features plans for 12 decks, progressing from low ground-huggers to more complex structures. Each plan is complete and ready to build and includes a full materials list. The construction details conform to most model building codes, but you should check them with your local building department and get proper permits before starting any work.

Each deck is designed for a specific site but can be adapted to many different locations. Even if you do not plan to build a particular deck, it is still worthwhile to look through the drawings. You may find the details useful for adapting another plan or even designing your own deck. The techniques and details that are presented for the simpler designs make the more complex designs easier to understand. If nothing else, the plans will help you see how footings, structural components, decking surfaces, railings, stairs, benches, and trim details come together to make a complete deck.

A successful deck does not have to be an intricate and complex structure. The simple shapes of the deck shown here blend well with the unadorned architecture of the house and fence. Its horizontal benches provide pleasant contrast to the vertical lines in the siding of the house and fencing.

QUICK DECK

Here is a simple deck made of sections you lay directly on the ground or on a level surface such as a patio, concrete pool skirt, or even a rooftop. Construction is as simple as it gets. Boards called "sleepers" sit on an existing firm surface. Two by four cleats run across the sleepers and 2×4s nailed across the cleats create the walking surface. The deck's low profile creates a sense of intimacy with the surrounding garden. You can change its shape and size by rearranging the sections to meet your needs.

Because the sections have no structural system tying them together, they require a level area that is stable and uniformly flat. You may find that over time, the sections shift in relationship to each other. This problem can usually be solved by leveling the sections periodically, by toenailing the sections together, or by installing the deck over long sleepers. Of course, if your site sits on soil that is highly expansive (like that with a high clay content), or if your area suffers from significant frost heaves, this type of deck may not be

MATERIALS LIST

For 12 sections, set on sleepers

	Quantity	Material	Size
Base	198 sq ft	landscape fabric (for weed control)	
	1 cu. yd.	gravel	
Sleepers	2	2×4s	12'
	2	2×6s	12'
Decking and Cleats	38	2×4s	12' (cut into 35½" pieces)
Screws	10 lbs	#8×2" deck screws, HDG (hot-dipped, galvanized)	

appropriate. Be sure to check with local building officials to make sure that what you have in mind is allowed.

THE 3×3 DECK SECTIONS

You can build the sections for your deck in almost any size or shape. The basis for this deck is a 3-foot-square section. This size is large enough to cover a good-sized area quickly, yet light enough to be easy to carry and install. The 3-foot section also goes together quickly. If you make the sections much smaller, it will take much more sawing and assembly to finish your deck.

BUILDING THE SECTIONS

MATERIALS: Use pressure-treated lumber rated for ground contact for the sleepers and cleats. For the decking, use either pressure-treated lumber or a durable wood like cedar or redwood. Since they span almost 30 inches, the deck boards should be a structural grade of lumber for maximum strength. (If you're using a lesser grade of wood, you may want to add a third cleat between the other two.)

SAFE HANDLING AND CUTTING OF PRESSURE-TREATED LUMBER

Pressure-treated (PT) lumber is toxic and should be handled with care. Here are a few precautions to follow when working with it:
■ Wear gloves, a long sleeve shirt, and long pants to keep the dust away from your skin.
■ Wear a dust mask and goggles when cutting PT wood.
■ Vacuum up all the dust and dispose of it properly. Do NOT use the saw dust for mulch or compost.
■ Wash up thoroughly after working and before eating or drinking.
■ Wash your work clothes separately from other laundry.
■ Do not burn scraps.

ASSEMBLY: To construct each section, cut the 2×4s into 35½-inch lengths. Build a simple spacing jig as shown. Place nine of the 2×4s inside the jig, with their best faces down. Lay the two cleats on top, flush with the ends of the decking boards, and screw the pieces together. If you have trouble with the screws splitting the wood, drill pilot holes first, each slightly smaller than the diameter of the screws.

After assembling the sections, nail spacers to the cleats, as shown, to provide uniform spacing between sections. Some sections will not need spacers, so you may wait to attach the scraps until you decide on a final configuration.

CONSTRUCTING 3-BY-3 MODULES

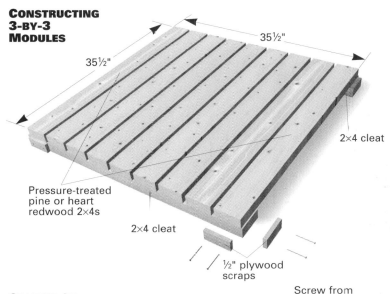

35½"
35½"
2×4 cleat
Pressure-treated pine or heart redwood 2×4s
2×4 cleat
½" plywood scraps

SPACING JIG

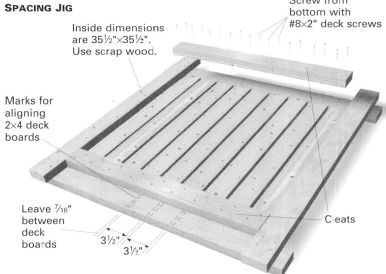

Inside dimensions are 35½"×35½". Use scrap wood.
Screw from bottom with #8×2" deck screws
Marks for aligning 2×4 deck boards
Leave 7/16" between deck boards
3½"
3½"
Cleats

QUICK DECK
continued

INSTALLING THE DECK SECTIONS ON THE GROUND

A wood deck that is placed directly on the ground will not last indefinitely, even under ideal conditions. But if you follow the methods outlined here, you should get years of service from your deck.

SITE PREPARATION: The most important feature of this deck's construction is the surface it rests on. Choose a site that drains well. Your deck won't last long if it sits on ground that stays damp for extended periods of time. Excavate a shallow depression and fill it with a 3-inch layer of gravel or crushed rock. To control weeds, line the excavation with a layer of landscaping fabric before putting down the gravel. See page 43 if you'd like to add a concrete or brick border around the excavation.

INSTALLATION: The sections are attached to a series of eight sleepers which lie directly on the gravel. The sleepers help keep the sections in line and level to one another. Lay out string lines to guide placement of the sleepers and sections. Because work will proceed from the center outward, lay out the middle first rather than the edges. Level the bed as best you can with a rake. Place the sleepers, as shown, and add or remove gravel as necessary to level them. Set the assembled sections on sleepers, starting in the center and working outward. The spacers attached to the edge of the cleats will help maintain consistent gaps between the sections. For extra rigidity, toenail the sections to the sleepers.

INSTALLING THE DECK OVER A PATIO

To cover an existing patio or pool skirt, place the wooden sections directly on the paving—no sleepers are required. For a permanent, slip-proof installation, attach the perimeter sections with exterior construction adhesive. To give the deck a slim profile, build it from 1-inch-thick material, but use four cleats for added stiffness.

SLEEPER SYSTEM FOR INSTALLING MODULES ON THE GROUND

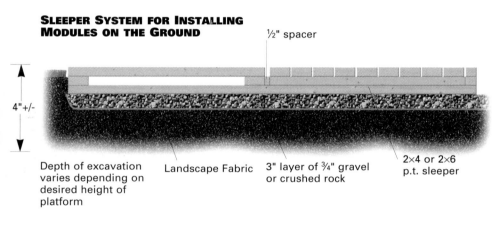

½" spacer

4"+/-

Depth of excavation varies depending on desired height of platform

Landscape Fabric

3" layer of ¾" gravel or crushed rock

2×4 or 2×6 p.t. sleeper

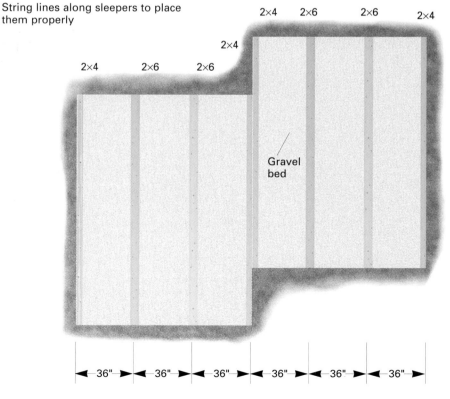

String lines along sleepers to place them properly

2×4   2×6   2×6   2×4   2×4   2×6   2×6   2×4

Gravel bed

36"   36"   36"   36"   36"   36"

INSTALLING DECK SECTIONS ON A ROOF

Rooftops offer an exciting option for outdoor living, and a modular deck system is the ideal candidate for such applications. Sections can be built at a more convenient location and transported to the rooftop, and they can be moved for roof maintenance. In a multi-unit dwelling, this might be an ideal project to approach as a cooperative venture, pooling resources and efforts with your neighbors to develop a pleasant outdoor space that you can enjoy together.

PREPARATION: Before starting, make sure the roof will support the weight of the deck. Many residential roofs are designed to support only their own weight (plus some snow load in colder climates). A roof intended as living space must be able to support an additional 30 or 40 pounds per square foot live load. Hire a professional consultant to determine if your roof is strong enough and to recommend structural changes if it isn't. The roof should be in sound condition and should have a slope of at least ¼-inch per foot so that puddles won't form.

Another consideration is access. It could be a simple matter of changing a window into a door. On the other hand, you may have to build a stairway or roof hatch, which may be more of a bother than building the deck elsewhere. Because walking directly on the roof can damage it, be sure the access leads directly to your deck. You also need to consider safety requirements, such as railings and protection from nearby power lines. And if you're thinking about gardening, you'll need a water faucet handy.

CONSTRUCTION: The sections in this plan are larger. They better distribute the load and are less likely to shift around. They use 2×6s instead of 2×4s, but are constructed the same way. The cleats are set in from the edge of the section rather than flush with it (see page 39) but this is simply for the sake of appearance.

INSTALLATION: The sections can be set directly on most roof surfaces. Sweep any roof gravel away first, and put strips of 45-pound felt under the cleats. Lay each section in place, and presto…instant deck. The sections will slope the same as the roof. Shim them every 3 feet, if desired, to level the deck.

A 3' BY 6' DECK MODULE

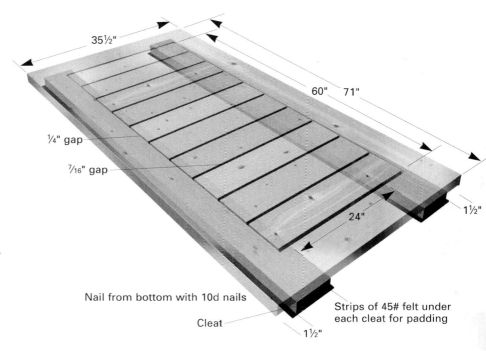

35½"

60" 71"

¼" gap

7/16" gap

24"

1½"

Nail from bottom with 10d nails

Cleat

1½"

Strips of 45# felt under each cleat for padding

12'

12'

A GROUND-LEVEL DECK

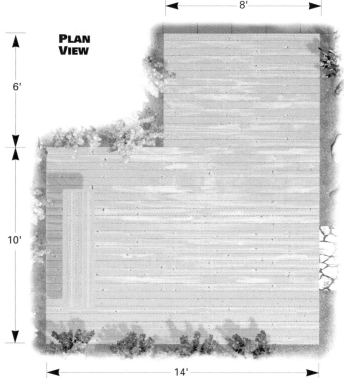

PLAN VIEW

8'

6'

10'

14'

This simple ground-level deck can be adapted to a variety of settings, including installations directly on the ground or over an existing patio. Sleepers run the entire length of the deck and decking runs across them for the entire width of the deck. Because this construction ties the deck into a single piece, there's no need for the cleats used in the **Quick Deck** on page 38.

Despite its simplicity, the L-shaped deck shown here makes an ideal transition area between the house and lawn. It provides a usable space away from the main traffic corridor, where a table or a pair of lounge chairs invite casual relaxing.

By lowering the deck into a shallow excavation and edging it with a masonry or concrete border, you can give it a touch of refined elegance. A wood surface that is level with the ground creates a dignified and dramatic landscape element.

BUILDING THE DECK

This deck was designed to be built directly on or below grade. For a long lasting deck, choose a site that drains well, and use pressure-treated wood that is rated for ground contact. You can alter the size and shape of this deck very easily by changing the lengths of the decking boards and the lengths and spacing of the sleepers.

SITE PREPARATION: Lay out the perimeter of the deck and excavate. For a deck surface that is flush with the surrounding grade, dig down 8 inches, and pour a concrete retaining border as shown in **Options for Borders**. For a deck that sits slightly above grade, a 3-inch-deep excavation is plenty. After excavating, lay down a layer of landscape fabric to control weeds, and spread a 3-inch-thick layer of gravel.

CONSTRUCTION: Cut the 4×4 sleepers to length and lay them on the gravel bed as shown in **Laying Out Sleepers**. The sleeper spacing on this deck is 42 inches, which requires the strength of 2×6 decking boards. If you use 2×4s or smaller deck boards, add more sleepers. Space sleepers for 2×4 decking no more than 24 inches apart; for 1-inch decking, no more than 16 inches apart.

Screw the decking boards to the sleepers with #8×2½-inch deck screws, two per sleeper. A layout line strung above each sleeper will help maintain a nice, straight line of screws.

TRIM AND FINISH: For a flush deck, place the border before building the deck. With an above-grade deck, you can add a wooden fascia as a finishing touch, as shown in **Options for Borders**. After all the construction is finished, stain or paint the deck to suit your taste.

MATERIALS LIST

Element	Quantity	Material	Length
Base	200 sq ft	landscape fabric (for weed control)	
	1.75 cu yd	¾" gravel	
Sleepers	2	4×4s	10'
	3	4×4s	16'
Decking	12	2×6s	8'
	20	2×6s	16'
Screws	10 lbs	#8×2½" deck screws, HDG (hot-dipped, galvanized)	
Border options			
A. Fascia	2	2×4s	6'
	1	2×4	10'
	1	2×4	14'
	1	2×4	16'
	1	2×4	18'
B. Concrete	1 cu yd	concrete	
	120'	1×8 (for forms)	
C. Brick	½ cu yd	concrete	
	360	paver bricks	
		mortar	

OPTIONS FOR BORDERS

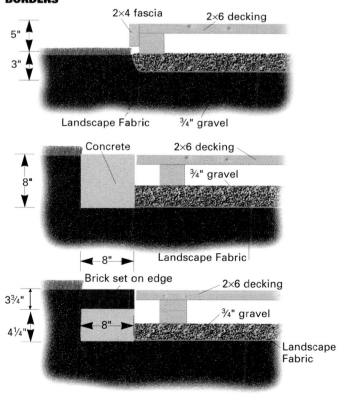

2×4 fascia 2×6 decking
5"
3"
Landscape Fabric   ¾" gravel

Concrete   2×6 decking
¾" gravel
8"
8"   Landscape Fabric

Brick set on edge   2×6 decking
3¾"   ¾" gravel
4¼"   8"
Landscape Fabric

LAYING OUT SLEEPERS

4×4 pressure treated sleepers

2×6 decking

6" ◄ 32" ► ◄ 42" ► ◄ 42" ► ◄ 42" ► 4"

REFURBISHING AN OLD PATIO

MATERIALS LIST

	Quantity	Material	Size
Footings	23 cu ft	concrete (for 8 piers 10" dia. × 36" and 8 footings 18" dia. × 8")	
	8	metal post anchors	
	16	⅜"×4½" carriage bolts with nuts and washers	
Sleepers	2	4×4s	8'
	4	4×4s	16'
		assorted shims and scrap blocks	
	1 tube	exterior construction adhesive	
Decking	16	2×6s	14'
	18	2×6s	10'
Fascia	2	2×8s	8'
	1	2×8	14'
Screws	10 lbs	#8×3½" deck screws	
Nails	1 lb	12d HDG common	

Although patios can be a useful and pleasing design element for most landscapes, many are too small to be of much use. If you'd like to expand your patio—or replace an aging one—covering it with a larger deck is far easier and faster.

The deck featured in this plan is for a condominium with a small yard and a correspondingly small patio. By expanding the outdoor living area, the deck makes the limited space much more usable and enjoyable. It also provides a strong focal point for the yard and creates an inviting transition between outside and inside.

BUILDING THE DECK

SITE PREPARATION AND FOOTINGS: A concrete or masonry patio is an excellent base for a deck, and it requires no special preparation, even if it is in marginal condition. If you want to extend your deck beyond the patio, however, you must provide bearing for the outside end of the sleepers. If the patio is fairly level, you may be able to prepare a gravel bed beyond the patio and lay sleepers directly on it (see page 40).

More likely, the patio slopes significantly (more than ¼ inch or so per foot) away from house, making it difficult to level the sleepers properly. In this case, you'll need more of a formal foundation for the outside ends of the sleepers. As shown, this involves pouring concrete piers and footings. (See page 19.) Lay out the piers, dig the holes, then form and pour the piers. Because the sleepers will bear directly on the piers, with no posts, it is critical that the piers all are level with each other. The easiest way to ensure this is to form and pour your own piers, rather then installing precast units.

SLEEPERS: Lay out the sleepers as shown in the **Framing Plan.** Level each sleeper periodically with shims, nail the shims to the bottom, and then attach the sleepers to the patio with exterior construction adhesive.

This plan uses 4×4 sleepers because they also act as beams. Make them from pressure-treated or naturally durable stock like redwood or cedar. Note that when placing sleepers on a sloped patio, the sleepers must run parallel with the slope so that they don't become dams that trap water.

FASCIA AND DECKING: Nail 2×8 fascia boards to the exposed sides and ends of the sleepers to give the deck a finished appearance. Screw the decking to the sleepers with #8×3½-inch deck screws. Drive two screws per board into each sleeper. It is best to lay out all the boards first so you can get the spacing just right.

FRAMING PLAN

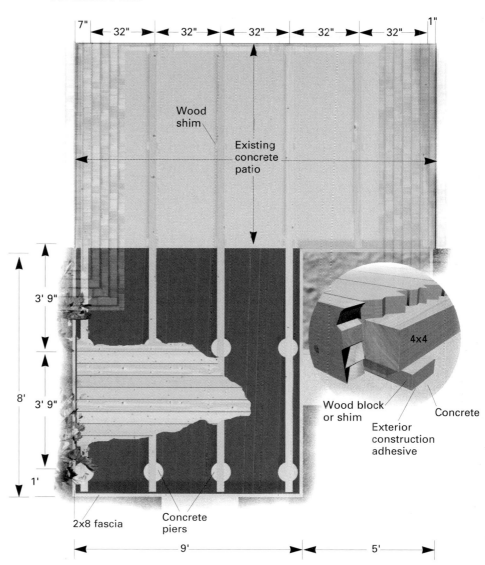

SECTION

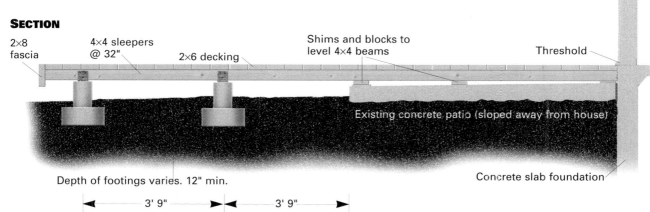

A SIMPLE GARDEN PLATFORM

PLAN VIEW

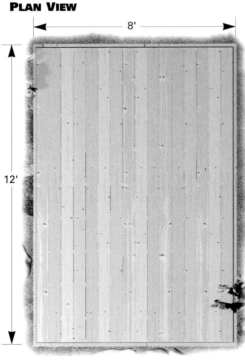

This freestanding deck is a permanent, raised platform that can be installed anywhere in a level yard. It is an ideal solution for a problem area, such as a drab corner where nothing seems to grow. Use it as a retreat, as a dining area, or as a fantasy platform for children's play. It is high enough to provide some detachment from other areas, and yet low enough that it appears to sit on the ground.

Because it is a simple rectangle, this deck must be located carefully so that its straight edges are oriented along an existing visual axis or axes. Otherwise, its size and strong form can make it look out of place. Even when it is carefully aligned with existing features, it can appear forced if the landscape already has an abundance of geometric forms. The easiest solution to this problem is to soften the deck's edges with plantings. Another solution is to add a meandering pathway of curved pavers leading to the deck.

BUILDING THE DECK

This deck is intended to be as low to the ground as possible. Since it isn't attached to the house, you may be able to reduce the clearance even more—check your local codes.

You achieve the low profile by hanging the joists between rather than on top of the beams and by using fairly small structural members (2×6s). This limits the width of the deck to approximately 8 feet, but you can widen it by adding a third beam.

LAYOUT AND FOOTINGS: To keep this deck low to the ground, the joists are hung between the beams, rather than set on top of them. When you lay it out, note that the outside edges of the piers are flush with the outside edges of the beams. Set up your batterboards as shown on page 16 and lay out lines to mark the outside edge of the pier. Dig the holes and pour the footings into the bottom of the hole. While the concrete is still wet, set form tubes for the piers with their inside edges tangent to the layout lines. Level the tubes carefully because the beams bear directly on top of the piers. Pour the piers, and while the concrete is still wet, imbed anchor bolts about 2 inches from the outside edge so that 5½ inches of the bolt are exposed.

BEAMS AND JOISTS: For a deck this close to the ground, the wood for the joists and beams should be suitable for ground contact, and all the hardware should be galvanized. Hold the beams in place on top of the piers and mark them for the anchor bolt holes. Drill a recess in the beam to hold a washer and nut, then drill bolt holes slightly oversize with a ⁹⁄₁₆-inch bit.

Bolt the beams in place and nail on the joist hangers as shown in the **Framing Plan**. Cut the joists to length, leaving a ¼-inch gap between the ends of the joists and the beams to avoid trapping moisture. Note: The end joists are 7 inches longer than the others and are nailed directly to the beam ends.

DECKING, FASCIA, AND FINISH: Screw the decking to the joists. Use two screws per joist in each board. The ends of the decking should be flush with the edges of the beams. Miter the ends of the 2×10 fascia boards and nail the boards to the outside of the platform, creating a skirt that keeps out debris, and helping the deck appear to hug the ground. If the deck is more than 10 inches above grade, provide a step. Finish the deck as desired with stain, paint, or natural weathering.

MATERIALS LIST

	Quantity	Material	Size
Footings	18 cu ft	concrete (for 6 piers 10" dia. × 36" and 6 footings 18" dia. × 8")	
	6	½" anchor bolts	
Framing			
Beams	2	4×6s	12'
Joists	10	2×6s	8'
Decking	17	2×6s	12'
Fascia	2	2×10s	8'
	2	2×10s	12'
Nails	2 lbs	joist hanger nails	
	5 lbs	16d HDG common	
Screws	7 lbs	#8×3½" deck screws	

FRAMING PLAN

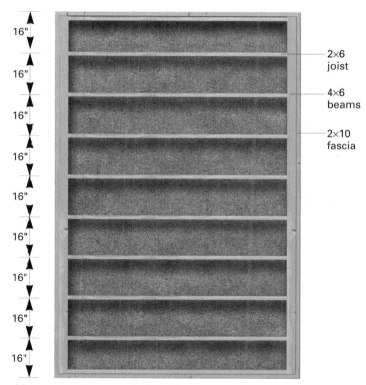

16" (×8)

2×6 joist
4×6 beams
2×10 fascia

Measurements are made from the center of each joist or are "on center"

SECTION

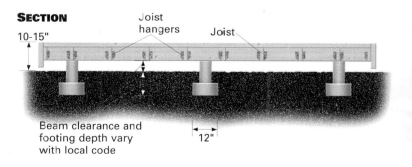

Joist hangers
Joist
10-15"
12"

Beam clearance and footing depth vary with local code

A SIMPLE GARDEN PLATFORM
continued

FRAMING PLAN

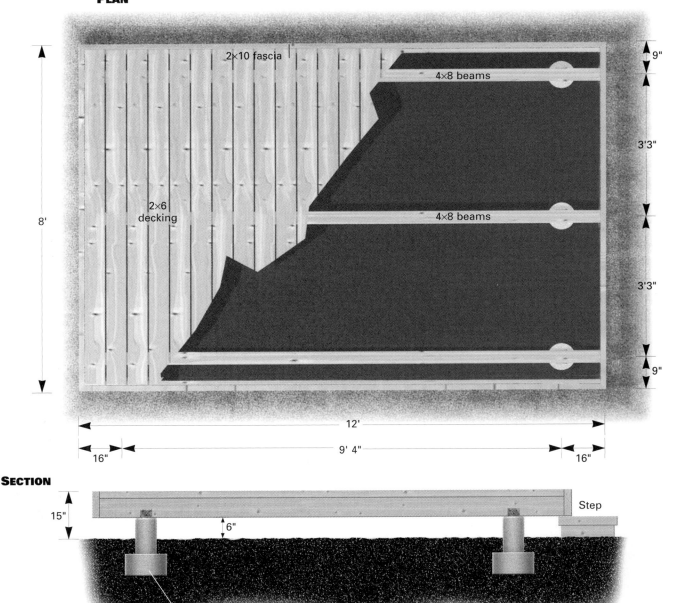

2×10 fascia

4×8 beams

2×6 decking

4×8 beams

9"

3'3"

3'3"

9"

8'

12'

9' 4"

16"

16"

SECTION

15"

6"

Step

Depth varies with
local codes

A SIMPLE VARIATION

The structural system for this deck consists of only three beams—no joists are necessary. The beams are 4×8, so you need only two footings for each one. You can change the size of the deck by lengthening the beams or by adding new beams to widen it. With this system, it is possible to make large platforms set low to the ground.

LAYOUT AND FOOTINGS: The foundation for this variation is similar to that for the original plan, but because the beams are set in from the perimeter, you can center the piers under the beams instead of setting them flush with the edges. All piers should be level with one another, because the beams rest directly on them.

BEAMS AND DECKING: Bolt the beams to the top of the piers. Screw the decking to the tops of the beams. Install the 8-foot boards, letting the ends extend beyond the edge of the deck. Trim them to length—7 feet 9 inches—preferably along both sides to produce neat, straight edges. The 7-foot, 9-inch length allows for an 8-foot fascia.

PLAN VIEW

FRAMING PLAN

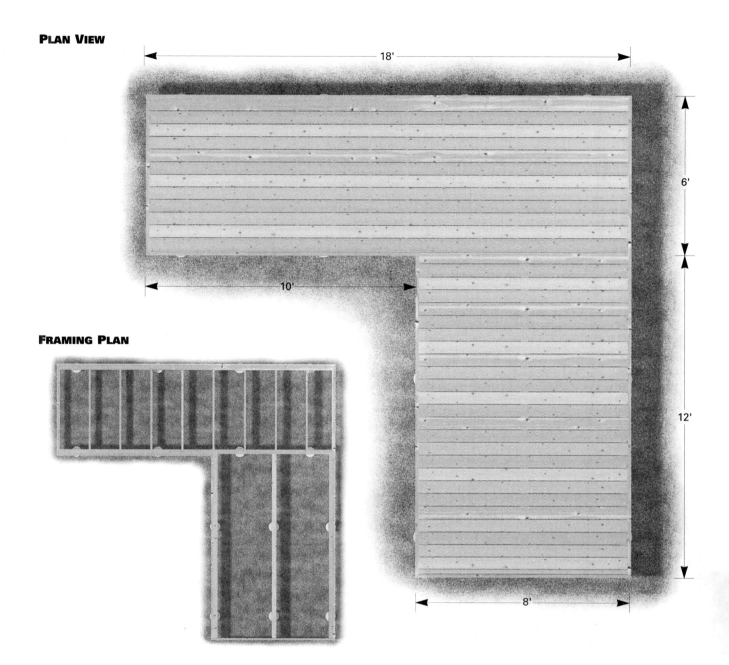

If you'd like to squeeze a few extra inches into your deck, use longer fascia and leave the decking at its full 8 feet.

FASCIA AND FINISH: On this deck the fascia is more than decorative. It also stabilizes the over-hanging ends of the deck boards. Rather than face nail the fascia to the ends of the decking, you'll get a nicer looking result if you screw a 2×4 cleat to the inside of the fascia boards. Then you can screw down through the decking just as if you were screwing into another joist.

Because this deck uses deeper beams, it is 15 inches high and requires a low step. Running such a step along one entire side makes a nice bench for sitting, or displaying plants.

AN L-SHAPED COMBINATION

This deck is really two decks similar to those on the preceding 3 pages. One section is supported by two 18-foot beams placed 6 feet apart, with 2×6 joists hung between them on 24-inch centers. See **Framing Plan**, above. The other section is supported by three 12-foot beams that are set perpendicular to the first two beams. One end of each 12-foot beam is supported by a beam hanger attached to the side of one of the 18-foot beams. Note that the middle footings for the 12-foot beams are not actually centered, but are offset toward the 18 foot deck.

A HILLSIDE DECK

This deck features an extremely versatile and widely-used construction system. Its foundation, like that for many of the decks in this book, consists of poured concrete piers, sunk in the ground below frost level. Metal brackets, cast into the tops of the piers, anchor wooden posts which rise to support wooden beams. The beams then carry the floor joists and decking. By varying the size and spacing of the posts, beams, and/or joists, you can design almost any size deck that will still carry the necessary loads.

This style of construction is appropriate for flat sites as well as sloping ones. This versatility comes from using posts to carry the beams rather than resting the beams directly on top of the piers. Because the posts are easily cut, the piers don't have to be level to one another.

The deck featured here is freestanding—that is, it doesn't rely on a house or other structure for support, although it could easily be adapted to do so. In many cases, however, it is easier to build a freestanding deck so you don't have to worry about how to tie it to the existing building. This is especially true for decks that are fairly low to the ground. The additional material cost will be minimal.

PLAN VIEW

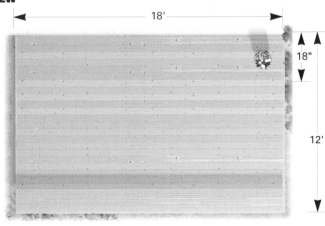

Because a hillside deck is freestanding, you can put it almost anywhere in the yard. The version shown here is tucked into a corner of the yard. Construction of the deck and bench are exactly as described in the rest of this project. The steps are a separate construction tucked under the deck. These steps and others are explained in Stairs and Steps, pages 28-31.

BUILDING THE DECK

In the drawing on the opposite page, the deck is resting on a gentle slope. The same structure could easily be adapted for steeper slopes by lengthening the posts and increasing the footing depths. Railings are required along any side of the deck that is more than 30 inches above the ground (check your local building code for the exact requirements). For gentle slopes, a bench may be sufficient protection, as shown. You may also want to consider adding stairs for access to the ground below. For more information on building stairs, see pages 28-31.

LAYOUT AND FOOTINGS: You'll need four string lines to lay out this deck—one to mark one end of the deck and the others to represent one edge of each beam. The steeper the slope the more difficult the layout will be because all measurements have to be made along a horizontal plane rather than along the slope. Set batter boards and stretch mason's line between them to make the layout. Measure along the beam lines to locate the footings. Drive stakes to mark the holes, and temporarily remove the lines so you can excavate.

When excavating for footings on a slope, dig the holes slightly deeper (2 or 3 inches for gentle slopes) than the code requirements for level ground Always measure the depth of the hole from the downhill edge. Place the forms in the holes and pour the footings and piers. As you set the forms, make sure that all the forms are roughly at the same level. It is more critical, however, that the metal post brackets are in line. Restring your layout lines and use them to position the anchors in the wet concrete.

POSTS, BEAMS, AND JOISTS: Cut the posts about 6 inches longer than necessary and bolt them to the top of the piers. If the posts are not made of pressure-treated lumber, you should soak their bottoms in a preservative first. When the posts are in place, plumb them and brace them temporarily with lengths of 2×4 that run diagonally to the ground.

Mark the tops of the uppermost posts for level and cut the posts to length. Use these posts as a reference to mark the remaining posts and cut the remaining posts to length as well. Bolt the beams to the posts, aligning beam ends with the layout line that marks the end of the deck.

Toenail the 2×6 joists to the beams and nail blocking in between the joists along the center beam. Snap chalk lines along both ends of the joists to mark the long edges of the deck. The chalk lines should be square to the end joists. Trim the joist ends to make a straight, clean edge.

DECKING AND FASCIA: Before attaching the deck boards, bolt the 2×8 bench uprights in place along the joists as shown and described in **Bench Details** on pages 52-53. Provide support for the decking boards under the bench by nailing a wood cleat onto the side of each upright opposite the joist it is bolted to. Screw the deck boards to the joists using two screws per deck board per joist.

A HILLSIDE DECK
continued

When you get to the 2×8 bench uprights, either notch a long deck board to fit around them or cut short lengths of decking to fit in between.

Once the decking is in place, nail the fascia boards around the outside edge of the deck, keeping the fascia's top edge flush with the deck surface. Miter the corners for a more finished look.

BENCH DETAILS: The built-in bench featured in this plan is very sturdy and gives a simple, clean look to the deck. As mentioned earlier, the bench uprights are installed first, before the decking is screwed in place. When you install the 2×8 uprights, be sure that their tops are all level and that they are all equidistant from the joist edges. The easiest way to get them all level is to mark each one exactly 18 inches from the top end and align this mark along the top edge of the joist when bolting it. Clamp the uprights to the joists to hold them in place as you drill the bolt holes.

After the decking is in place, assemble the rest of the bench. Cut off the corners of the cleats so the ends will be hidden behind the 2×4 trim as shown. Bolt them in place so they are centered on the 2×8 upright and level. Nail the 2×2s to the cleats to make the seats. Toenail the pieces in place so the nails don't show. You may find it necessary to predrill the holes to keep the pieces from splitting. When all the 2×2s are in place, trim their ends. Install the 2×4 trim boards around the bench's perimeter, mitering the corners for a more finished look.

MATERIALS LIST

	Quantity	Material	Sizes
Footings	11 cu ft	concrete (for 9 piers 8" dia. × 36" and 9 footings 18" dia. × 8")	
	9	metal post anchors	
		18⅜"×4½" carriage bolts with nuts and washers	
Framing			
Posts	1	4×4	8' (for 6 short posts)
Beams	3	4×6s	18'
Joists	10	2×6s	12'
Blocking	2	2×6s	10' (cut into 9 22½" pieces)
	9	metal post/beam connectors	
	18	⅜" × 4½" carriage bolts with nuts and washers	
Decking	24	2×6s	8'
	24	2×6s	10'
Fascia	2	2×8s	12'
	2	2×8s	10'
	2	2×8s	8'
Bench			
Uprights	2	2×8s	10' (cut into 10 23½" pieces)
Upper & Lower Cleats	4	2×4s	8' (cut into 20 15" pieces)
Seat	21	2×2s	8'
Trim	4	2×4s	10'
Bolts	20	⅜"×5" carriage bolts w/ nuts and washers	
	20	⅜"×3½" carriage bolts w/ nuts and washers	
Nails	5 lbs	8d HDG finish nails (for bench)	
	7 lbs	16d HDG common nails	
Screws	10 lbs	3½" deck screws	

FOOTING AND FRAMING PLAN

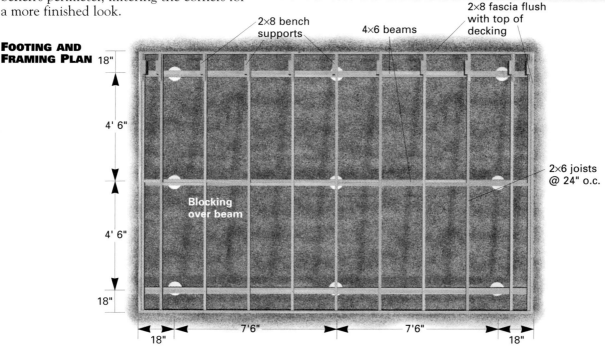

END VIEW

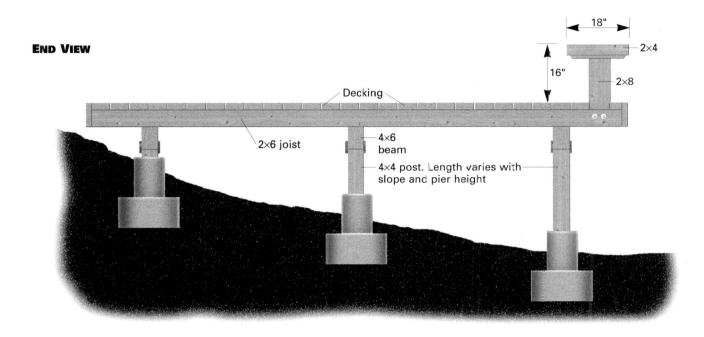

18"

2×4

16"

2×8

Decking

2×6 joist

4×6 beam

4×4 post. Length varies with slope and pier height

DOWNHILL SIDE

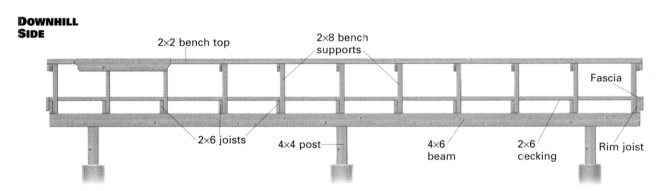

2×2 bench top

2×8 bench supports

Fascia

2×6 joists

4×4 post

4×6 beam

2×6 cecking

Rim joist

BENCH DETAIL

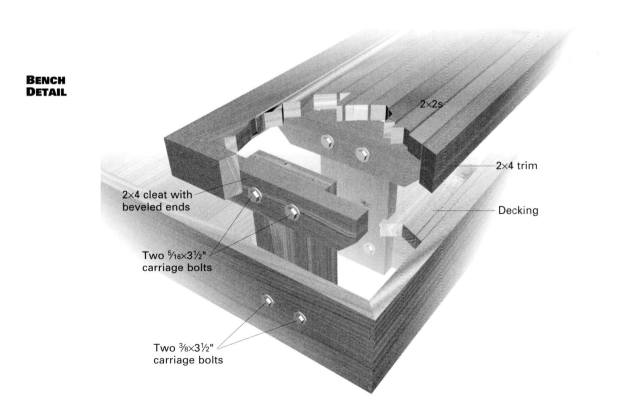

2×2s

2×4 trim

Decking

2×4 cleat with beveled ends

Two 5/16×3½" carriage bolts

Two 3/8×3½" carriage bolts

A MULTILEVEL DECK

On a sloped site, a deck that follows the slope has several advantages. The stepped design keeps all parts of the deck close to the ground, eliminating the need for railings. Multiple levels can also help define areas of the deck for specific uses such as dining or socializing. Stepped or multilevel decks are particularly effective for sites that slope up away from the house or main areas of the yard. Multiple levels help make the deck look and feel accessible without being prohibitively tall.

In order to keep the deck as low to the ground as possible, this design combines two different structural systems. For the lower platform, the deck boards are placed directly on a series of 4×6 beams which are supported by poured concrete piers. Because there are no posts between the beams and the piers, the piers must all be level with one another.

The upper platform is supported by a beam-and-joist structure. Posts on piers raise the platform to a height approximately 28 to 30 inches above grade. This is generally the maximum height allowed for decks without railings.

The two levels and the intermediate step are all tied together structurally. Not only does this economize on the use of materials, but it makes it easier to keep all the pieces level in relationship to each other. The vertical spacing between the levels is also planned with standard framing lumber in mind. The rise of each step is 7½"— the actual width of a 2×8.

To keep the lower level as low to the ground as possible, you can excavate shallow trenches between the piers that will carry the low beams. These trenches help provide the necessary clearance between the ground and the beams.

BUILDING THE DECK

Talk to your lumber dealer about what grades of weather-resistant material are available. This design calls for spans that are near the maximum for the size of lumber specified. You should always try to use the best grade of materials you can get, or you'll need to reduce the spans.

LAYOUT AND FOOTINGS: Start laying out the deck by setting batter boards and stretching a line to indicate the center of the long beam (shown at the left edge of the **Footing and Beam Plan**). Set batter boards, and stretch a second line for the piers that will carry the ends of the short beams. (Those across the bottom of the drawing.) The lines should cross directly over the center of the corner pier and should be perpendicular to one another. Measure from the intersection point to lay out the positions of the various piers along the two lines. Drop a plumb bob from the lines to mark the centers of the holes and drive a stake into the ground to mark each pier.

Set a third pair of batter boards and stretch a line for the second long beam. Stake the pier centers along this line as you did for the others. Finally, set batter boards and string lines for the remaining three sets of piers. Measure and stake as usual.

Take down the strings, leaving the batter boards in place for now. Dig the holes for the footings, put the forms in place, and fill them with concrete. When the concrete hardens,

PLAN VIEW

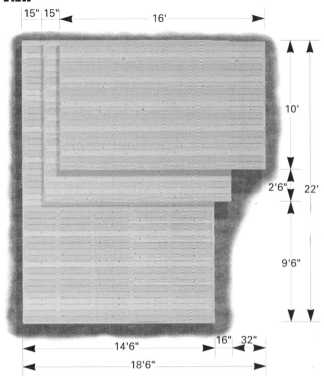

SAFETY NOTE

There is an important safety consideration to keep in mind when designing a multilevel deck. Steps can be difficult to see, especially outside where sun glare and dappled shade patterns can hide what would otherwise be obvious. The strong pattern of the deck boards can also camouflage changes in level, especially one-step drops.

The deck featured on these pages solves that problem by making a two-step change in levels and by trimming the steps with a 2x4 fascia. The narrow edge of the fascia helps break up the surface pattern of the decking, while a shadow line underneath the board adds definition to the step's surface. You can also run the decking boards in different directions for each level and/or provide a handrail to make the steps more obvious. In situations involving people whose eyesight isn't good, you can even paint the edges of steps with a bold color to make them stand out.

MATERIALS LIST

Element	Quantity	Material	Finished Sizes
Footings	2 cu yards	concrete (for 20 piers 8" dia. × 36" and 20 footings 18" dia. × 8")	
	20	metal post anchors	
	40	⅜"×4½" carriage bolts with nuts and washers	
Framing			
Posts	1	4×4	4' (for 4 short posts)
Beams	2	4×6s	8'
	4	4×6s	10'
	2	4×6s	14'
	2	4×8s	16'
Joists	1	2×6	16'
	2	2×6s	8' (for 6 30" joists)
	9	2×8s	10'
	2	2×8s	12' (for 6 48" joists)
	2	2×8s	14'
	3	2×8s	16'
Blocking	1	2×6	12' (for 5 28½" pieces)
	2	2×8s	8' (for 8 22½" pieces)
Joist Hangers	10	2×6s	
	13	2×8s	
Decking	47	4×6s	16'
Fascia	2	2×4s	10'
	2	2×4s	12'
	4	2×4s	16'
Nails	4 lbs	joist hanger nails	
	10 lbs	16d HDG common nails	
Screws	20 lbs	#8×3½" deck screws	

A MULTILEVEL DECK

continued

restring the layout lines and center the forms for the piers directly under the lines. Double check to make sure the distance between the piers is right, and level the tops of the piers with each other. If necessary, trim the tops of the forms to level them. Fill the forms with concrete. Set the post anchors into the wet concrete, centered under the layout lines. Measure to make sure the distance from anchor to anchor is correct.

BEAMS AND JOISTS: Install the 4×6 beams first, drilling and bolting them in

place. Cut posts to support the 4×8 beams and bolt them to the remaining four piers. Install the 4×8 beams on top of these posts. Note: One end of each 4×8 beam rests on one of the 4×6 beams.

FRAMING: The narrow part of the lower deck is framed with short 2×6 joists hung between the beams on joist hangers. For air circulation, cut the joists about ¼-inch short to provide a gap at each end. Nail the joist hangers to the joists first. Next, hold them in place and nail the hangers to the beam or stringer. This way you can be sure the top of the joist will be flush with the top of the beam.

To frame the step, hang short 2×8 joists from the side of one of the 4×8 beams with joist hangers. The other ends are attached to a rim joist which rests on the ends of the short 4×6 beams. Two long 2×8 joists resting on the short 2×6 joists you installed previously complete the stair framing.

Frame the upper deck by toenailing the 2×8 joists to the 4×8 beams. Nail a rim joist to both ends of the joists. Since the rim joists' surfaces will be visible, be careful not to mar it. Install blocking between the upper deck joists and the short, lower deck joists.

DECKING AND FASCIA: Screw the deck boards to the lower deck. Start flush at the end and work toward the step. You may have to rip the last board to fit. Start the step and platform from the edge closest to the lower platform. Start the first board flush with the rim joist.

Nail the fascia boards to the edges of the two decks and the steps as shown in the **Section Through Side Steps** on page 58. Miter the pieces where they meet at the corners. The fascia makes the steps easier to see by breaking up the pattern of the decking and providing a shadow line on each step.

FOOTING AND BEAM PLAN

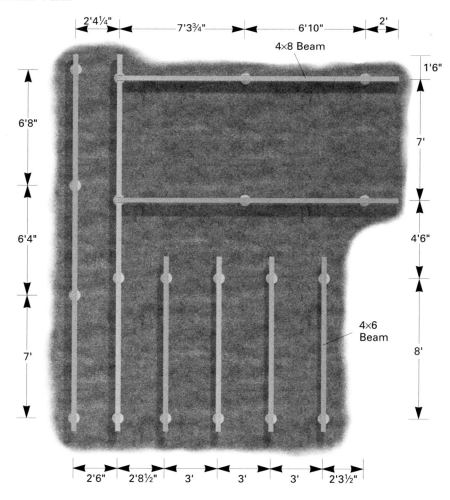

2'4¼" 7'3¾" 6'10" 2'

4×8 Beam

1'6"

6'8"

7'

6'4"

4'6"

7'

4×6 Beam

8'

2'6" 2'8½" 3' 3' 3' 2'3½"

FOOTING AND FRAMING PLAN

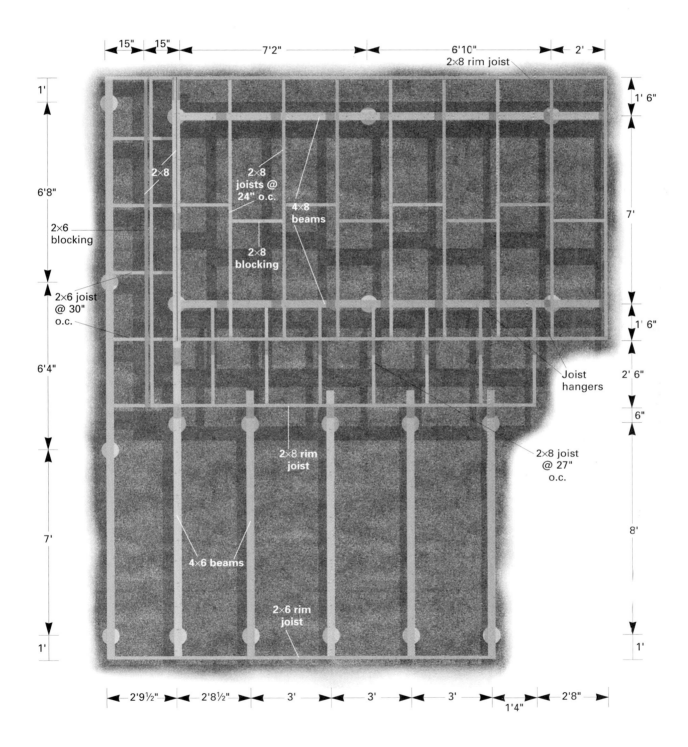

A MULTILEVEL DECK

continued

SECTION THROUGH CENTER OF DECK

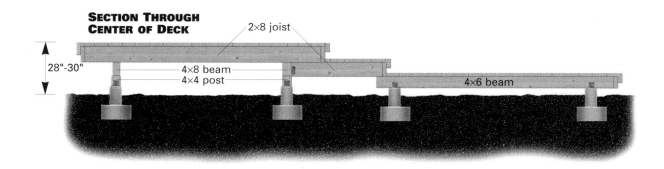

2×8 joist

28"-30"

4×8 beam

4×4 post

4×6 beam

SECTION THROUGH SIDE STEPS

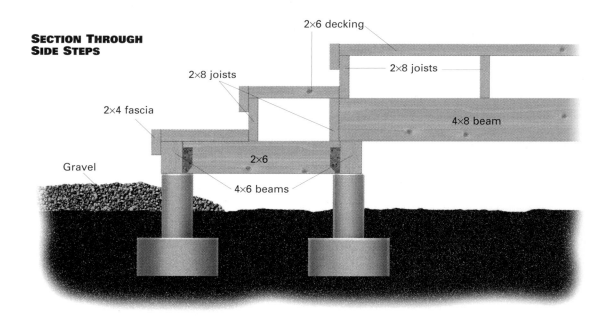

2×6 decking

2×8 joists

2×8 joists

2×4 fascia

4×8 beam

Gravel

2×6

4×6 beams

OPTIONAL FASCIA DETAIL

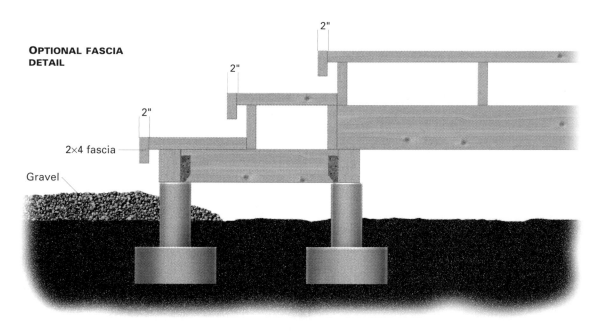

2"

2"

2"

2×4 fascia

Gravel

DECK PATTERN VARIATION

If you have longer deck boards, you may want to play with the pattern of the decking. The variation shown here has a more formal appearance brought on by the mitered corners of the decking. The **Footing and Framing Plan** shows the same footing locations, beam structure, and upper platform joists as the plan on page 54. The major changes are the addition of short joists between the outer beams of the lower platform and between the joists along the left side of the upper step.

MULTILEVEL DECK VARIATION

Dimensions do not include fascia

FOOTING AND FRAMING PLAN FOR VARIATION

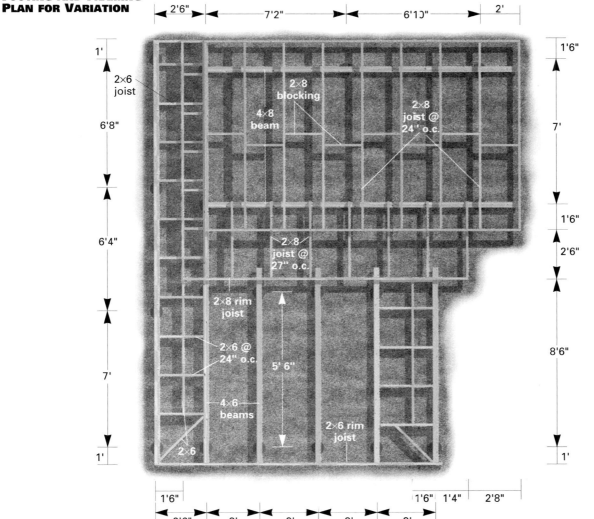

AN ENGAWA

**PLAN
VIEW**

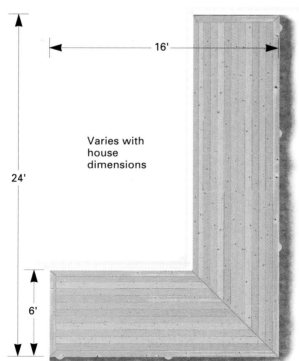

16'

24'

6'

Varies with
house
dimensions

An engawa is a Japanese-inspired deck that is really a simple walkway around the house—a transition area between out and in. Because it is at floor level, it is very convenient and inviting, giving the feeling that you can be in your garden without even leaving your room.

Construction is fairly straightforward. The deck is attached to the house via a ledger that is bolted to the house's frame. One end of the joist is nailed to the ledger; the other is nailed to a beam. Decking covers the joists, and footing supports the beam.

As shown, this deck is intended for a house with a wood floor that is 12 to 18 inches above grade. If your floor is higher, you can raise the deck by resting the joists on top of the beam rather than hanging them from its side. You could also raise the deck by lengthening the support posts. Note, however, that most codes require that decks taller than 30 inches have a railing for safety.

BUILDING THE DECK

Make sure the ground slopes away from the house at least ½-inch per foot and that any downspouts in the area have leaders to carry the water beyond the deck's edge. The house itself should be in sound condition. Repair any damaged siding and paint any new wood that will be covered by the deck.

LAYOUT AND FOOTINGS: Stake and stretch a string line 6 feet away from the house. Measure along the string and lay out the piers with stakes. Take the string down, leaving the stakes, and dig the holes for the piers. (Check with your local utility company to make sure you won't hit any power or gas lines before excavating. Also be careful not to disturb any plumbing or drain lines.)

Place the forms and pour the footings and piers. Set the metal post anchors in the wet concrete with the outside edges directly under the string line.

Backfill around the piers and spread a layer of landscape fabric on the ground to keep weeds from growing under the deck. Weigh down the fabric with gravel or rocks.

FOOTING AND FRAMING PLAN

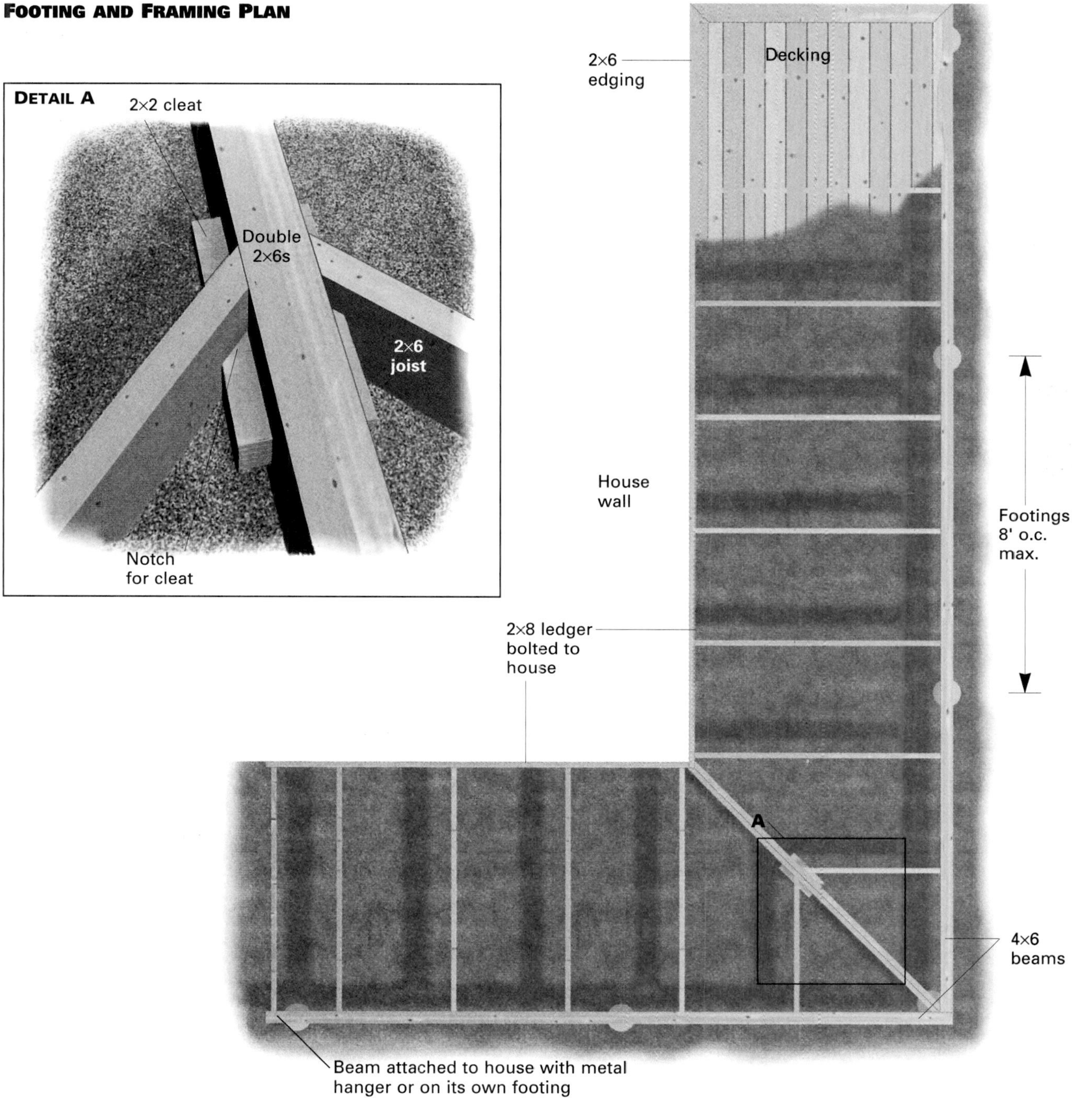

DETAIL A
2×2 cleat
Double 2×6s
2×6 joist
Notch for cleat

2×6 edging
Decking
House wall
2×8 ledger bolted to house
Footings 8' o.c. max.
A
4×6 beams
Beam attached to house with metal hanger or on its own footing

AN ENGAWA
continued

LEDGER, BEAM, AND JOISTS:

Unless your house is sided with plywood or other solid siding, you'll need to remove the siding to a level that is slightly above that of the deck. Measure 2½ inches down from the floor level and draw a level line along the sheathing to represent the top of the ledger. This allows a 1-inch drop from floor level to the top of the deck boards, a drop that keeps water from backing up into the house.

Bolt the ledger to the floor framing of the house, using galvanized lag bolts or carriage bolts and washers as shown in **Bolting a Ledger to a House** on page 63. Add flashing before reinstalling the siding above the ledger. Cut the posts that will support the beam so the top of the beam will sit 1½

FRAMING DETAIL

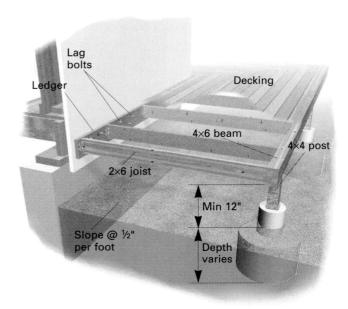

inches below the top of the ledger. This will pitch the deck slightly (¼-inch per foot) away from the house for drainage. Bolt the posts to the piers and the beams to the posts.

Install the joists between the ledger and the beam with joist hangers. When you cut the joists to length, make them about ¼ inch short to allow for air circulation at either end. At the corner, you'll need a doubled, diagonal joist as shown in the **Framing Plan** on page 61. Bevel the ends of the two joists and fit them individually. Nail them to each other with 8d nails and then nail them in place. Notch two short joists and attach them to the doubled 2×6 with cleats, as shown.

DECKING: The deck itself is made of a combination of 2×8s and 2×6s. The 2×8s form a frame that runs around the deck's perimeter. The 2×6s fill in the field. Start by cutting the 2×8s to outline the perimeter, mitering the ends at the corners. Attach the pieces with three 3½-inch deck screws per joist. Once the frame is in place, start filling in the middle with lengths of 2×6. The gap between the edges of the pieces should be slightly less than ¼ inch. Stagger the butt joints where the ends come together for a more pleasing look. Attach the boards with two screws per joist.

MATERIALS LIST

	Quantity	Material	Sizes
Footings	14 cu ft	concrete (6 piers 8" dia. × 36" and 6 footings (18" dia. × 8")	
	12	metal post anchors	
	36	⅜"×4½" bolts with nuts and washers	
Framing			
Posts	1	4×4	6' (for 6 short posts)
Ledgers	2	2×8s	10'
	1	2×8	8'
Beams	1	4×6	8'
	2	4×6s	16'
Joists	9	2×6s	12' (18 66¼" pieces)
	3	2×6s	8'
Joist hangers	38	2×6s	
Bolts	44	½"×6" lag screws or machine bolts for ledger (length varies with thickness of siding)	
	200	½" washers (extras are for spacers)	
Decking	1	2×8	8'
	1	2×8	10'
	4	2×8s	12'
	1	2×8	16'
	20	2×6s	8'
	10	2×6s	10'
	10	2×6s	12'
Nails	5 lbs	joist hanger nails	
	3 lbs	16d HDG common nails	
Screws	8 lbs	#8×3½" deck screws	

Framing Detail labels: Lag bolts · Ledger · Decking · 4×6 beam · 4×4 post · 2×6 joist · Min 12" · Depth varies · Slope @ ½" per foot

**BOLTING A
LEDGER TO
THE HOUSE**

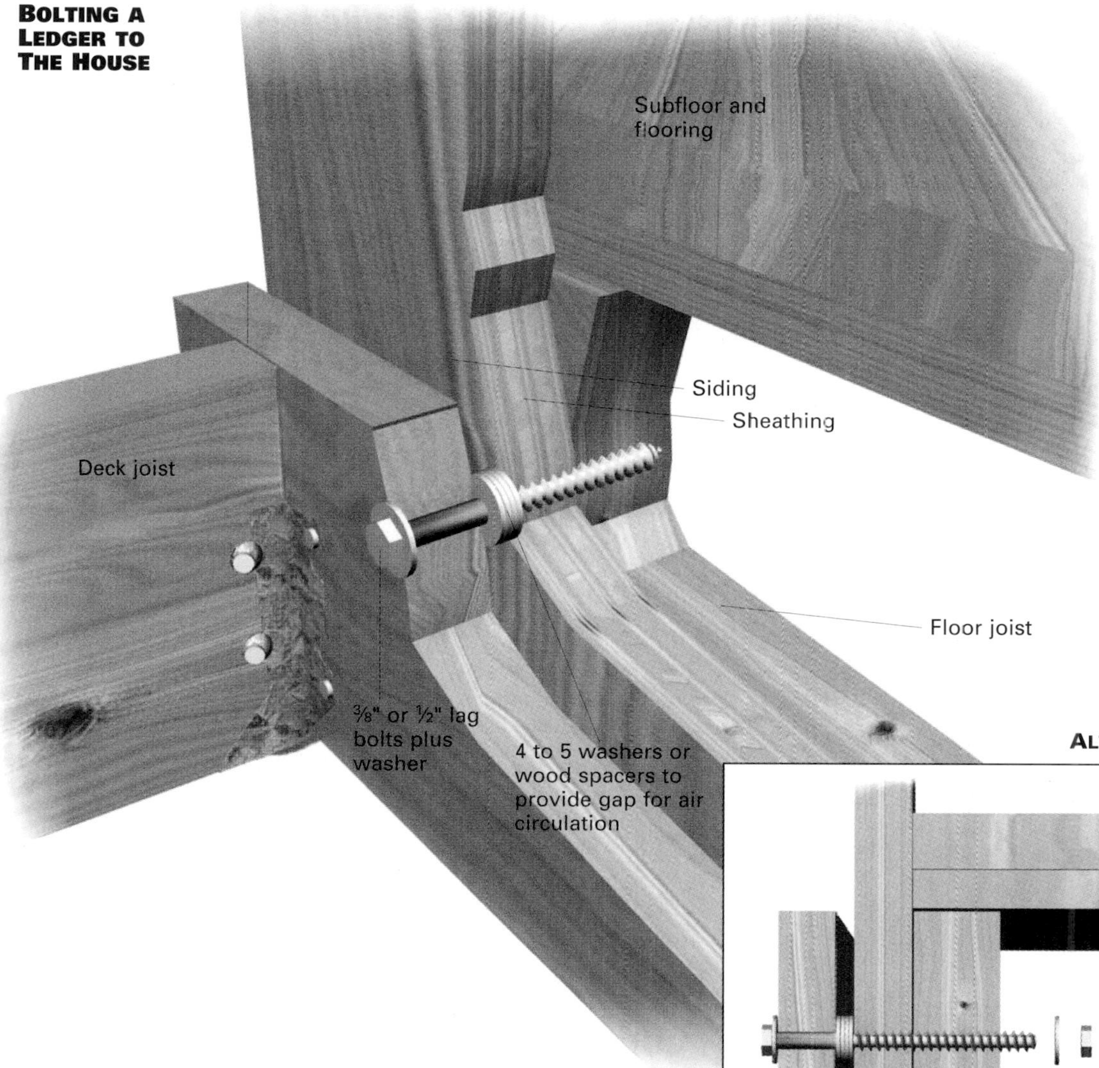

Subfloor and
flooring

Siding

Sheathing

Deck joist

Floor joist

⅜" or ½" lag
bolts plus
washer

4 to 5 washers or
wood spacers to
provide gap for air
circulation

ALTERNATE BOLTING

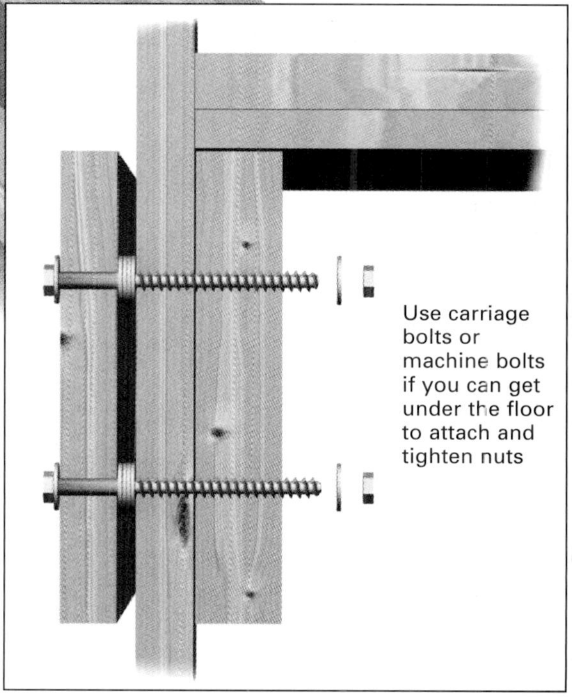

Use carriage
bolts or
machine bolts
if you can get
under the floor
to attach and
tighten nuts

**BOLT
SPACINGS**

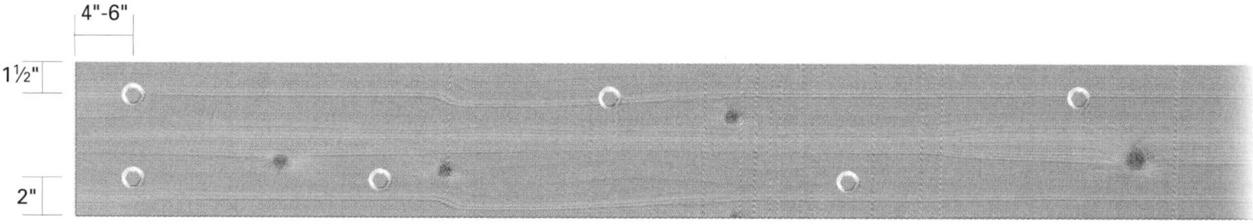

4"-6"

1½"

2"

Single bolting 16" to 24" o.c

A PLATFORM DECK WITH STEPS

For a home with a first floor that is several steps above ground level, this multilevel deck may make the perfect transition between house and yard. The design features a series of steps and platforms that cascade away from the doorway to the garden below. Because the height of this deck averages 20 to 30 inches above grade, it doesn't require railings, but it does use benches to help define some individual spaces.

The deck itself is free standing. It is supported on concrete piers sunk into the ground. 4×4 posts rise from the piers to carry 4×8 beams, which in turn support the joists and decking. Each of the two platforms uses two beams. A fifth beam, located where the platforms meet, carries some of the weight of each platform. This fifth beam shares oversized posts with beams for the upper platform. The two beams are bolted together for added stability.

Steps lead off both sides of the lower platform to the ground below. Depending on the drop, a simple box step (as shown to the right, above) may be enough, or you can build a conventional stairway (left) with stringers and treads. Two wide steps run the full length of the upper deck, providing seating and leading into the house. These stairs are the only part of the deck actually connected to the house. They are supported by a series of short joists, one end of which bears on the deck, the other is hung from a ledger board that is bolted to the house.

BUILDING THE DECK

LAYOUT AND FOOTINGS: Start your layout by stretching strings to represent the centers of the two beams for the upper platform. Use the house as a reference from which to measure. Once you have them in place, set the strings for the remaining beams at the proper angle (130 degrees), with a variation of the 3-4-5 triangle. Begin by tying a new string—for the shared beam—to batter boards about two feet beyond where you think each end of the beam will be. The point where the new string crosses the others is where two beams come together. Adjust the new string until the intersection point is properly

PLAN VIEW

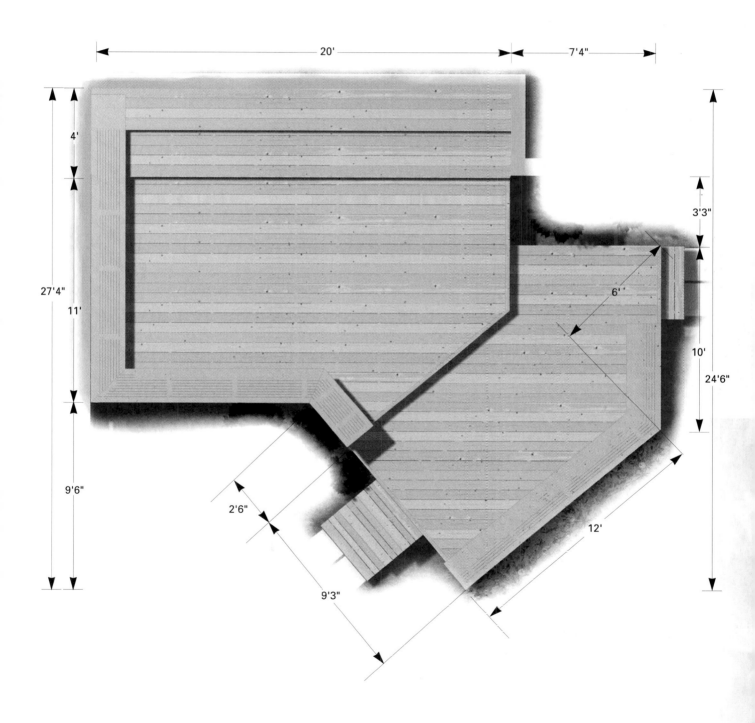

A PLATFORM DECK WITH STEPS

continued

located. Mark both strings at this point. Make another mark—on either of the strings—6 feet from where they cross. Mark the other string 8 feet from where they cross. Adjust the angle of new string until the distance between the marks equals 12 feet-9 inches. See the opposite page for an illustration of this technique. As you adjust the strings, make sure they continue to cross at the proper place. Stretch the strings for the other beams parallel to string you've just positioned.

Mark the ground for the footing holes, then remove the strings. Dig the holes, set the forms and pour the footings. Put the strings back on the batterboards to help locate the pier forms. Pour the piers and set metal post anchors in the wet concrete.

LEDGER: Locate the top of the ledger for the steps leading into the house 10 inches below floor level. This allows for rise of the stair plus 1½-inch thick stair treads and a 1-inch drop outside the door for weather protection. See pages 62–63 for more details on attaching ledger boards.

FRAMING AND DECKING: The deck's height is controlled by the length of the posts. Cut the posts 3 inches too long and bolt them to the piers. Use a transit or a water level to mark them at the proper level, using the top of the ledger as a reference. Mark the tops of the posts for the upper platform 15 inches below the top of the ledger. Mark those for the lower platform 22½ inches below the ledger.

After the posts are cut, bolt the beams in place. Install the joists and rim joists, starting with the lower platform and working your way up. Screw the deck boards to the joists, two screws per board per joist. Add the fascia to finish the process.

ACCESS STAIRS: Build stairs to the garden after the deck is finished. For one or two steps, build simple platforms as described on page 28. For a longer staircase, you'll need to build a regular staircase as described on page 30. Cut three stringers from

MATERIALS LIST

	Quantity	Material	Sizes
Footings	1 cu yd	concrete for 11 piers (8" dia. × 36") and 11 footings (18" dia. × 8")	
	11	metal post anchors	
	22	⅜"×4½" carriage bolts with nuts and washers	
Framing			
Ledger	2	2×8s	10'
Posts		4×4s	(varies with site)
	1	4×8	(length varies with site)
Beams	1	4×8	8'
	3	4×8s	10'
	2	4×8s	12'
	1	4×8	14'
Joists	11	2×8s	8'
	5	2×8s	10'
	10	2×8s	12'
	1	2×8	14'
	3	2×6s	8'
	1	2×6	10'
	8	2×6s	12'
Blocking	1	2×8	8' (cut into 22½" +/- pieces)
	1	2×8	10' (cut into 22½" +/- pieces)
	2	2×6s	8' (cut into 22½" +/- pieces)
Joist hangers	6	2×6s	
	11	2×8s	
Corner joist hangers	2	2×8	
	1	2×6	
Post to Beam Connectors	10	4×4	
	1	4×8	
Bolts	18	½" dia. × 5" lag bolts with 90 washers	
	44	⅜" dia. × 4½" carriage bolts with nuts and washers	
	6	½"×4" carriage bolts and washers	
	2	⅝"×10 carriage bolts with nuts	
Decking	42	2×6s	8'
	54	2×6s	10'
Fascia	2	2×4s	8'
	6	2×4s	10'
	2	2×4s	12'
	1	2×4	14'
Bench			
Uprights	3	2×12s	10' (cut into 24 14½" pieces)
Cleats	2	2×4s	12' (cut into 24 11¼" pieces)
Aprons	2	2×4s	16'
	5	2×4s	12'
	1	2×4	8"
Seat	2	2×4s	16'
	5	2×4s	12'
	1	2×4	8"
Stairs			
Stringer	1	2×12	12'
Treads	3	2×6s	12'
	3	2×4s	12'
Nails	3 lbs	joist hanger nails	
	25 lbs	16d HDG common nails	
Screws	30 lbs	#8×3½" deck screws	

FOOTING AND FRAMING PLAN

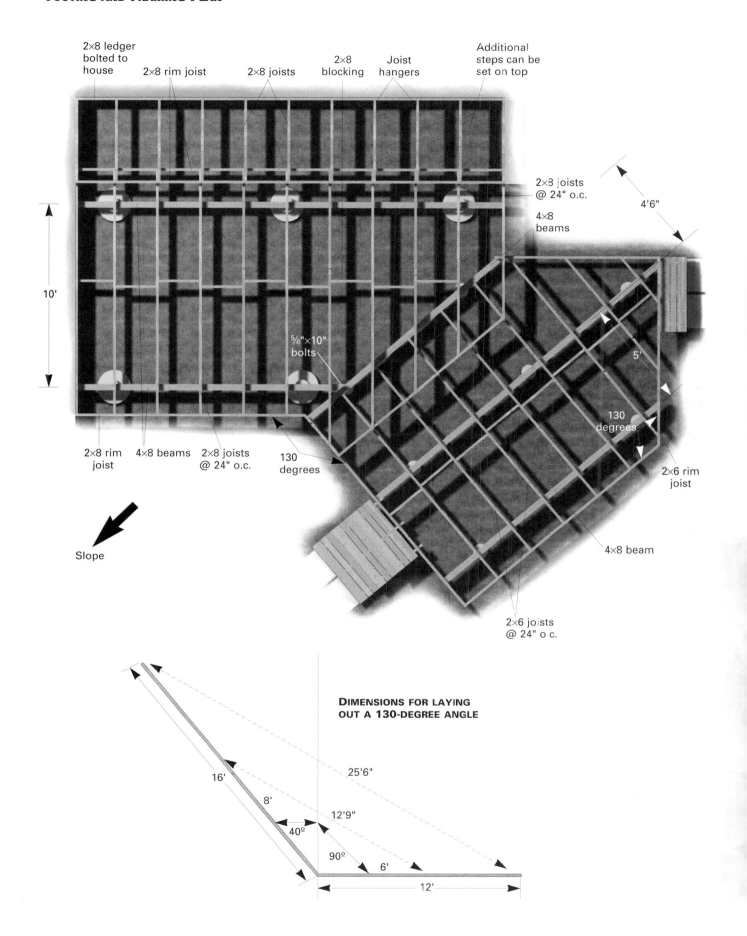

2×8 ledger bolted to house

2×8 rim joist

2×8 joists

2×8 blocking

Joist hangers

Additional steps can be set on top

2×3 joists @ 24" o.c.

4×8 beams

4'6"

10'

⅝"×10" bolts

5'

130 degrees

2×8 rim joist

4×8 beams

2×8 joists @ 24" o.c.

130 degrees

2×6 rim joist

4×8 beam

2×6 joists @ 24" o.c.

Slope

DIMENSIONS FOR LAYING OUT A 130-DEGREE ANGLE

25'6"

16'

8'

12'9"

40°

90°

6'

12'

A PLATFORM DECK WITH STEPS
continued

a 2×12 as shown in the **Stair and Bench Details**. The actual dimensions of your stair will vary with the site. However, it is important that all the risers be the same height (preferably the 7½ inches used elsewhere in the deck). Pour a concrete pad for the bottom of the stair. You can vary the height of the concrete to help even out the stair's rise. Bolt the stringers to the beams under the deck (the middle one will require some blocking) and screw the treads in place.

BENCHES: The benches on this deck are built in place. Start by cutting the pieces to size and then bolt the 2×4 cleats to all the uprights.

Lay out the location of each upright on the deck. Predrill the uprights. To make sure each upright is aligned properly, square it against the edge of the deck with a framing square and then toenail it in place. Set the nails carefully for a neat appearance.

After the uprights are in place, plumb them. Then screw the apron pieces to either side, using two screws per apron per upright. Note: The apron runs up onto the stair at the top of the deck and can be toenailed in place. Nail a line of 2×4s to the cleats along the outside edge to start forming the seat. Fill in the middle of the seat with 2×2s. Use nails as spacers to maintain an even gap between the pieces. You can toenail the pieces through their sides to keep the nails from showing if you want to. Stagger the end joints and miter the pieces at the corners.

FRAMING DETAIL

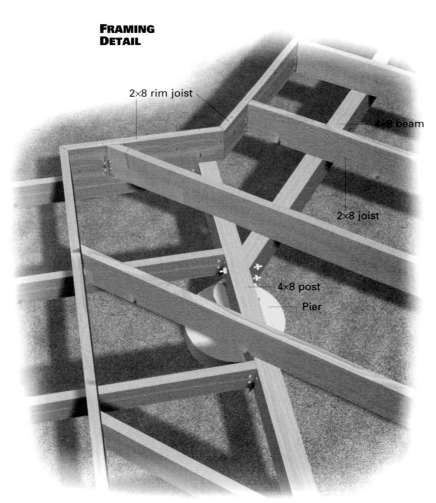

- 2×8 rim joist
- 4×8 beam
- 2×8 joist
- 4×8 post
- Pier

SECTION

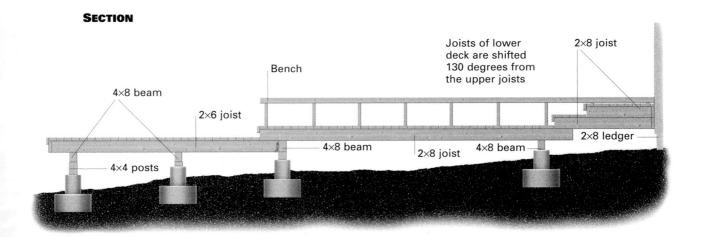

- 4×8 beam
- 4×4 posts
- Bench
- 2×6 joist
- 4×8 beam
- 2×8 joist
- 4×8 beam
- Joists of lower deck are shifted 130 degrees from the upper joists
- 2×8 joist
- 2×8 ledger

**STAIR AND
BENCH DETAILS**

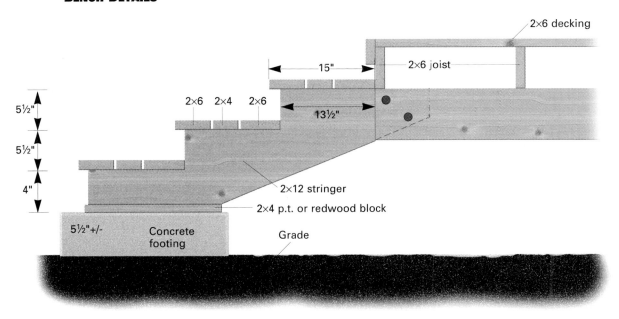

2×6 decking

2×6 joist

15"

13½"

2×6   2×4   2×6

5½"

5½"

4"

2×12 stringer

2×4 p.t. or redwood block

5½"+/-   Concrete footing

Grade

BENCH DETAIL

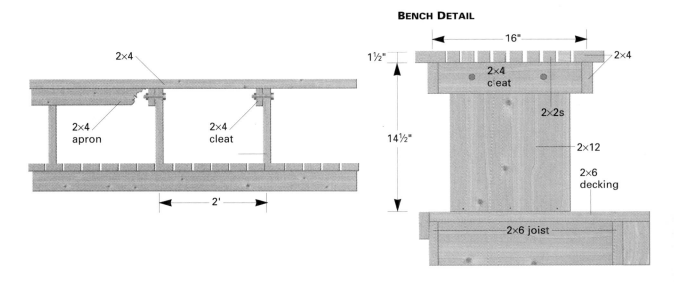

2×4

2×4 apron

2×4 cleat

2'

16"

1½"

2×4

2×4 cleat

2×2s

2×12

2×6 decking

14½"

2×6 joist

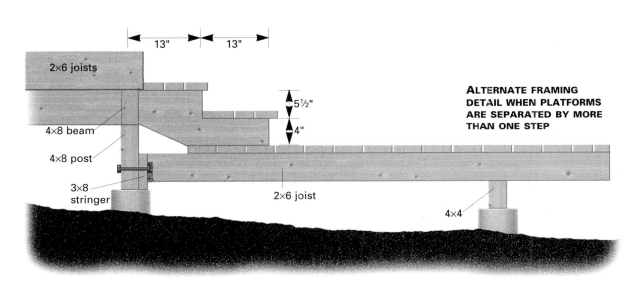

2×6 joists

13"   13"

5½"

4"

**ALTERNATE FRAMING
DETAIL WHEN PLATFORMS
ARE SEPARATED BY MORE
THAN ONE STEP**

4×8 beam

4×8 post

3×8 stringer

2×6 joist

4×4

A WRAPAROUND DECK

PLAN VIEW

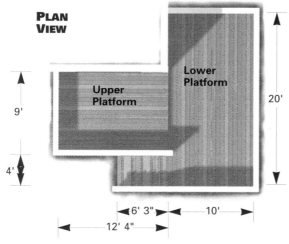

Upper Platform

Lower Platform

9'

4'

20'

6' 3"

10'

12' 4"

Despite its grand appearance, this deck is actually a simple two-level platform wrapped around a corner of the house. Like many of the other decks in this book, this deck consists of deck boards nailed to a series of joists which are supported by ledgers, beams, and posts. The solid railing that extends to the ground is a cosmetic detail added to help the deck blend in with the rest of the house. It also affords some privacy to anyone using the deck. Note how the trim and siding were designed to match the house and make the deck look as if it had always been a feature of the house.

BUILDING THE DECK

LAYOUT AND FOOTINGS:

Measuring from the house, stretch strings to lay out the piers according to the **Footing and Framing Plan**, page 67. The strings should represent the outside edges of the posts. It is critical to precisely locate the posts at the top of the stairs. These carry the double 2×10 that extends out from the house. Its location can't be adjusted.

Mark the pier locations, then remove the strings and dig the holes. Set forms in the holes and pour the concrete. Reset the strings, place the forms, and pour the piers. Place metal post anchors in the wet concrete with their outer edges flush with the strings. The piers should be approximately level with each other and as close to grade as possible so the siding can end as close to the ground as wanted. While you're pouring concrete, you may want to pour the landing for the stairs, too. For more information see **Stairs** on page 74.

LEDGERS, POSTS, AND BEAMS:

One side of each level of the deck is supported by a ledger bolted to the house. The other side is supported by beams bolted to posts. Snap a line 2½ inches below floor level on the house to indicate the top of the upper ledger. Snap a line for the top of the lower ledger on the adjacent wall, 7½ inches below the first line.

The upper ledger is a single 2×10. Bolt it to the wall even with its line. The lower ledger is slightly more complex. It starts as a single 2×10 bolted to the house. However, it extends past the house's corner, where it is paired with a second 2×10. This beam/ledger will be heavy and awkward to install, so get some help. Cut both 2×10s to length, and nail them together with three 8d nails every 16 inches. Erect the far post and brace it in position. Prop and temporarily nail the beam in place, and then level it and bolt it to the house and post. For more on installing ledgers, see pages 62–63.

MATERIALS LIST

	Quantity	Material	Sizes
Footings	1 cu yd	concrete for 12 piers (8" dia. × 36") and 12 footings (18" dia. × 8")	
	12	metal post anchors	
	24	⅜"×4½' carriage bolts with nuts and washers	
Stair Landing	.25 cu yd	concrete (7 cu ft) for 6"×36"×54" slab	
	2	anchor bolts for 2×4 cleat	
Framing			
Posts	15	4×4s	8'
Ledger	1	2×10	12'
Ledger/Beam	1	2×10	14'
	1	2×10	20'
Beams	2	2×8s	12'
	4	2×8s	10'
Joists	18	2×8s	10'
Blocking	4	2×8s	8' lengths
Ledger bolts	18	½" dia. × 6' lag bolts with 90 washers	
Post bolts	8	½" dia. × 3" lag bolts and washers	
Beam bolts	16	½" dia. × 7" carriage bolts with nuts and washers	
	10	½" dia. × 6" carriage bolts with nuts and washers	
	2	½" dia. × 11" carriage bolts with nuts and washers	
Joist hangers	2×8s	39	
Decking	40	2×6s	10'
	18	2×6s	12'
Stair Treads	2×6s	4	10' (for 5 steps)
	2×2s	2	10' (for 5 steps)
Railing and Skirts (68 lineal feet)			
Frame	27	2×4s	8'
	7	2×4s	10'
	2	2×4s	12'
	1	2×4	16'
Cap rail	1	2×6	8'
	5	2×6s	10'
	1	2×6	12'
Siding		Sheathing and/or siding material to cover 700 sq ft (460 on outside of deck, 210 on inside of railings + 5% waste)	
Trim	2	1×4s	8'
	10	1×4s	10'
	2	1×4s	12'
Flashing		6" wide by 68' long	
Nails	15 lbs	16d HDG common nails	
	5 lbs.	Joist hanger nails	
		Nails for siding and/or sheathing, depending on material used.	
Screws	17 lbs	#8×3½' deck screws	

A WRAPAROUND DECK
continued

Next, erect all the rest of the posts and hold them in plumb with temporary braces. Do not try to cut the posts to exact height until the deck platform is finished. Make a mark on each post level with the top of the ledger opposite it. Face nail the 2×8s for the beams together with two 8d nails every 16 inches. Prop the beams in place so their tops are flush with the mark on each post. Drill holes and bolt the beams to the post.

JOISTS AND DECKING: Install joists 24 inches on center, hanging them between the ledger and beams with joist hangers. On each level, there will be one odd-sized gap where the spacing doesn't work perfectly, but this is fine structurally. Install blocking for both levels. Install the deck boards so their edges are tight against the posts. Trim the single step with 2×4 fascia.

SECTION THROUGH BOTH PLATFORMS

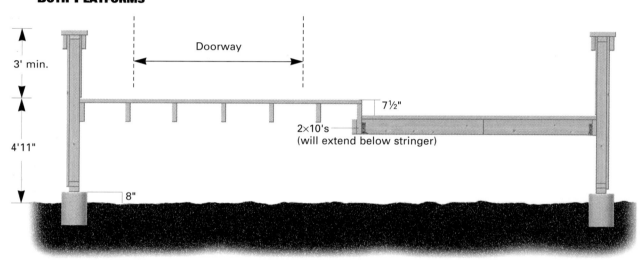

3' min.

4'11"

Doorway

7½"

2×10's
(will extend below stringer)

8"

SECTION THROUGH LOWER PLATFORM

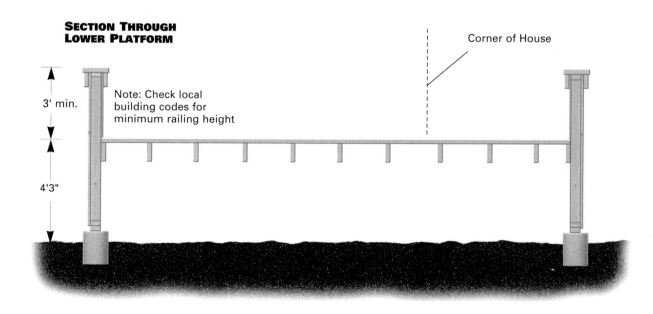

Corner of House

3' min.

Note: Check local building codes for minimum railing height

4'3"

FOOTING AND FRAMING PLAN

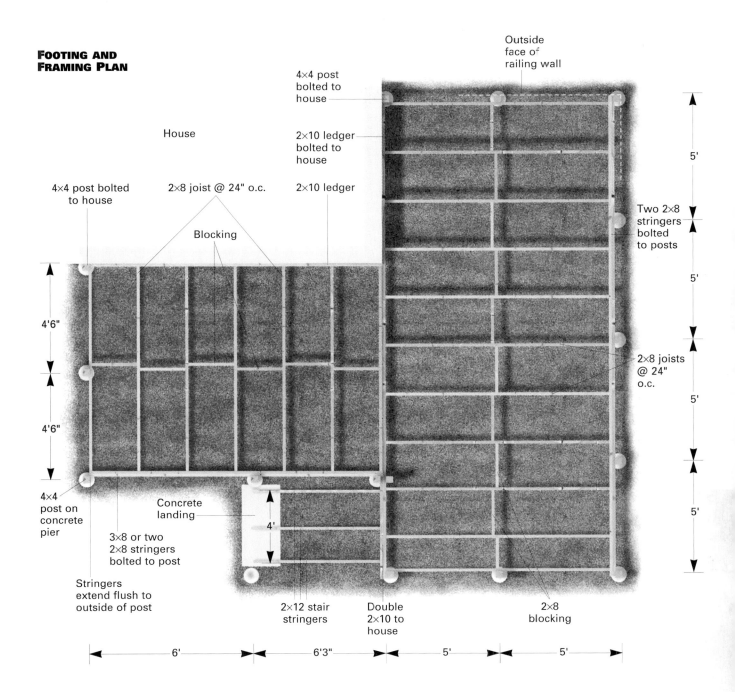

Outside face of railing wall

4×4 post bolted to house

House

2×10 ledger bolted to house

4×4 post bolted to house

2×8 joist @ 24" o.c.

2×10 ledger

Blocking

Two 2×8 stringers bolted to posts

4'6"

4'6"

2×8 joists @ 24" o.c.

4×4 post on concrete pier

Concrete landing

4'

3×8 or two 2×8 stringers bolted to post

Stringers extend flush to outside of post

2×12 stair stringers

Double 2×10 to house

2×8 blocking

5'

5'

5'

5'

6'   6'3"   5'   5'

A WRAPAROUND DECK
continued

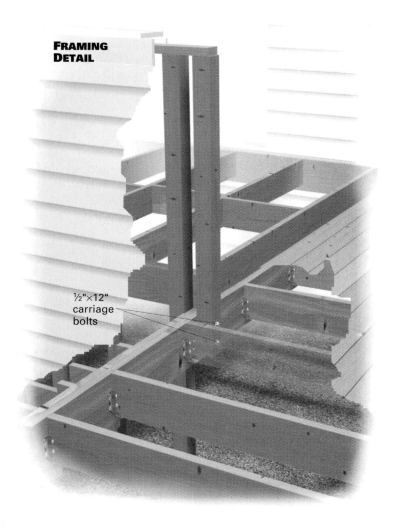

FRAMING DETAIL

½"×12" carriage bolts

STAIRS: While you are digging the holes for the footings, dig an 8-inch-deep hole about 3½ feet wide by 5 feet long for the stair landing. Fill the hole with 4 inches of gravel. Build forms for the landing with scraps of 2×10. Fill the forms with concrete and set anchor bolts for the cleat at the bottom of the stair before the concrete hardens.

To lay out the stair stringers, measure to find the total rise of the stairs (the distance from the top of the landing to the underside of the decking) and the total run (the distance from the outside of the stair cleat to a point 7 inches from the edge of the deck—the top step is considered part of the decking, not part of the stairs.) To find the depth of each tread, divide the total run by the number of treads you want. To find the height of each riser, divide the total rise by the number of desired treads plus one. Lay out and cut the stringers. (See pages 28–31 for more complete stair-building information).

Notch the stringers to fit over the cleat, then toenail them in place with 12d nails. Attach them to the double 2×10 beam with joist hangers.

Make the stair treads from two 2×6s separated by a 2×2. Depending on the tread width, there should be an overhang of about 1½ inches. You will find it easier to install the treads after the siding is in place. For air circulation and moisture control, leave a ¼-inch gap between the end of each tread and the siding.

STAIR DETAIL

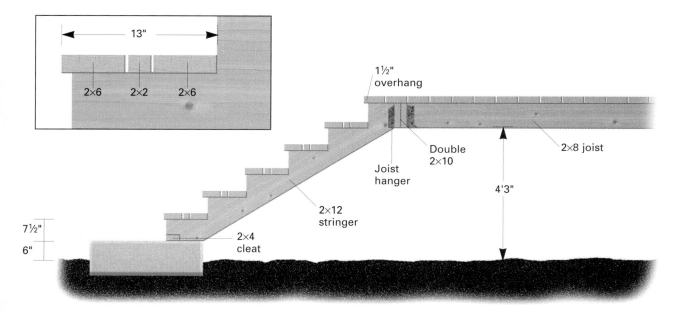

13"

2×6   2×2   2×6

1½" overhang

Double 2×10

Joist hanger

2×8 joist

4'3"

2×12 stringer

7½"
6"

2×4 cleat

RAILINGS AND SIDING: To finish the railing, cut the posts to length: 33 inches above the decking for 36-inch railings. Nail a 2×4 cap on top of the posts and 2×4 plates between the posts just above the piers. The plates are easier to install if you use metal connectors, such as fence framing clips. These are nailed to the posts and have pockets for holding the ends of the plates. If you do not use framing clips, toenail the plates to the posts. Measure and cut studs to fit between the bottom plate and the 2×4 cap. Nail them in place, 16 inches on center, and toenail them to the beams as well.

Nail sheathing or siding to the framework in the same way you would apply exterior siding (although building paper is not necessary). If you're using shingles, shakes, or stucco, you should install CDX or similar plywood sheathing first. Install horizontal wood siding or plywood siding directly to the studs. To prevent moisture from leaking inside the railing, place 15-pound felt or metal flashing over the top plate. Finally, install the 2×8 cap and 1×4 trim.

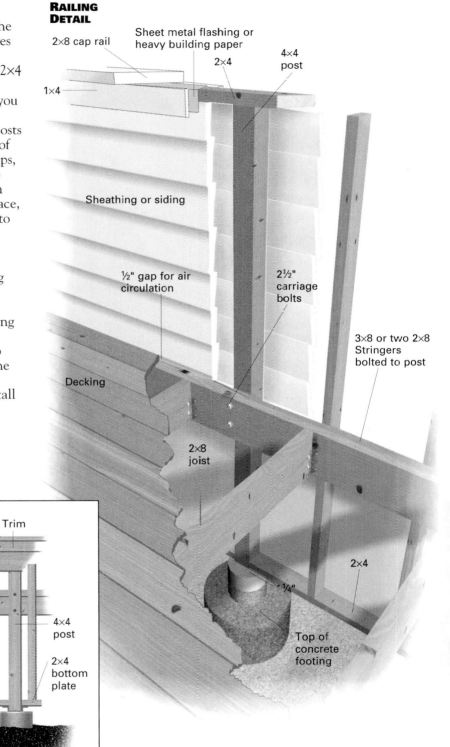

RAILING DETAIL

2×8 cap rail

Sheet metal flashing or heavy building paper

2×4

4×4 post

1×4

Sheathing or siding

½" gap for air circulation

2½" carriage bolts

3×8 or two 2×8 Stringers bolted to post

Decking

2×8 joist

2×4

¼"

Top of concrete footing

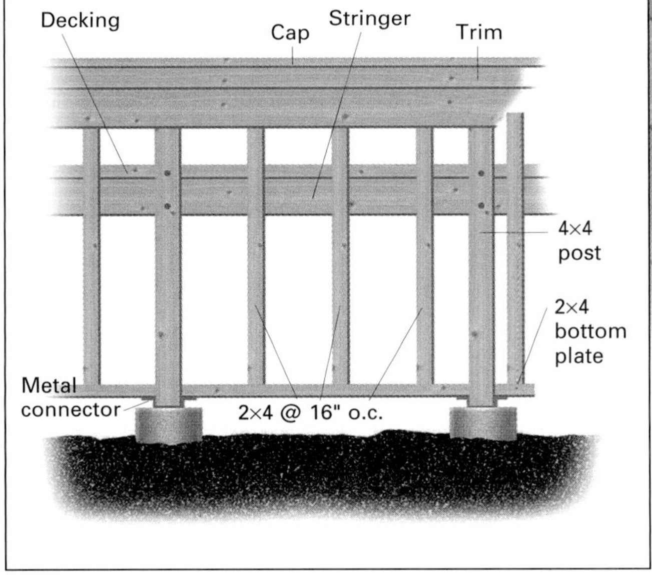

Decking   Cap   Stringer   Trim

4×4 post

2×4 bottom plate

Metal connector

2×4 @ 16" o.c.

A SPLIT-LEVEL DECK

This deck is really two adjacent decks—a large deck that sweeps into the yard, tucked under a smaller deck that is adjacent to the house. Arranging the decks like this has several advantages. The upper deck focuses on the house. It's at the same height as the house floor, and double doors make the deck seem like an extension of the interior. This portion of the deck sits tight against the house, which shades the deck on hot days. It's elevated just enough to provide a sense of security. It's narrow enough to provide a sense of intimacy.

The lower deck focuses on the yard. It sweeps out away from the house and is likely to be sunny when the rest of the deck is in the shade. It's large enough for a group of people, but the solid railing provides a sense of privacy.

Despite siding that makes this look more like a porch than a deck, the framing is fairly standard deck construction. The upper deck is a traditional deck tied to the house with a ledger. The posts which support the deck also support one end of the lower deck. The rest of the lower deck has its own system of piers and posts, joists and decking. If you look at the **Post and Framing Plan** on Page 79 you'll see, however, that instead of thick beams resting on posts, this deck has a system of thinner stringers bolted to opposite sides of the posts. The system tends to be a bit more rigid than beams, but you'll discover its primary advantage when you start lifting the lumber into position. A 2×8 stringer weighs exactly half as much as a 4×8 beam.

BUILDING THE DECK

LAYOUT AND FOOTINGS: Start laying out the deck by stretching a string parallel to the house through the centerline of the four posts that support the upper platform. Measure along the string and mark the center of each post. Three of these posts also support the lower platform. To begin laying out the lower section, stretch a second string across the first at the midpoint of the middle shared post. The angle between the strings should be 135 degrees. To check, measure out from the intersection point 6 feet on one string and 9 feet on the other. The distance between the end points should be 14 feet. Stretch three other strings parallel to the second to lay out the other lines of posts.

Dig holes and pour the footings and piers, setting metal post anchors in the wet concrete. The three shared posts are 4×6s. Place their anchors with the 6-inch side parallel to the house.

PLAN VIEW

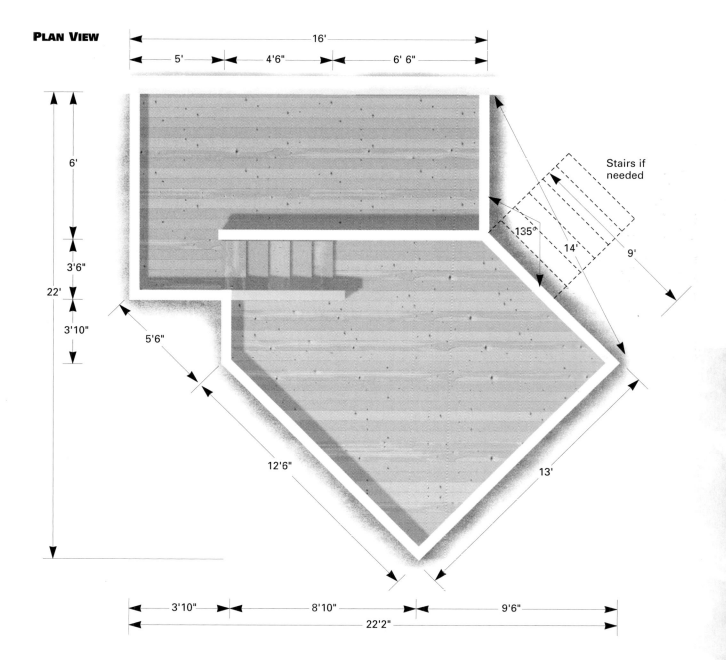

A SPLIT-LEVEL DECK
continued

LEDGERS, POSTS, AND STRINGERS:
Snap a chalk line for the ledger 2½ inches below the floor level. Bolt the 2×8 ledger to the house with its top edge even with the line. For more on installing ledgers, see pages 62–63. Bolt the posts to piers and brace them in position. Snap a line for the upper platform's double 2×8 stringer across the posts. The line should be 1 inch lower than the top of the ledger so that the deck slopes for drainage. Nail the 2×8s together and bolt them to the posts.

The stringers for the lower platform are set at two levels. The outer stringers should be 36 inches down from the top of the upper platform stringer, so that you can nail joists into them. The two inner stringers are 7½ inches lower, so that the joists can sit on them. Use a water level to transfer these marks from post to post. Bolt the stringers in

SECTION SHOWING BOTH PLATFORMS

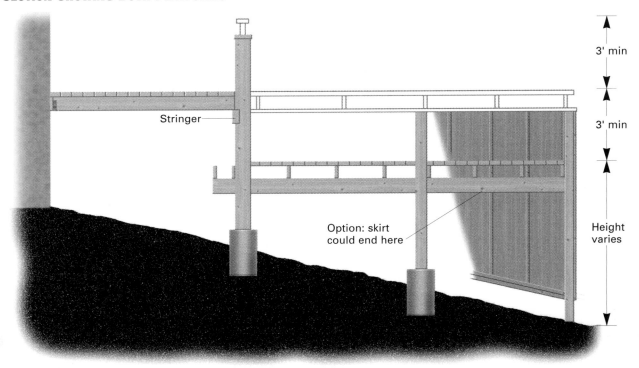

Stringer

Option: skirt could end here

3' min

3' min

Height varies

SECTION THROUGH STAIRS

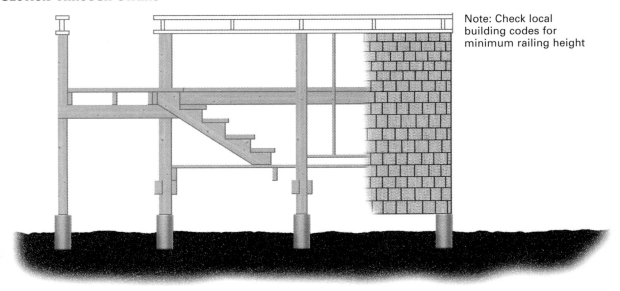

Note: Check local building codes for minimum railing height

POST AND FRAMING PLAN

Note: Framing at perimeter of deck is designed to accept framing system for solid railing extended to ground. Railing for framing is not shown here.

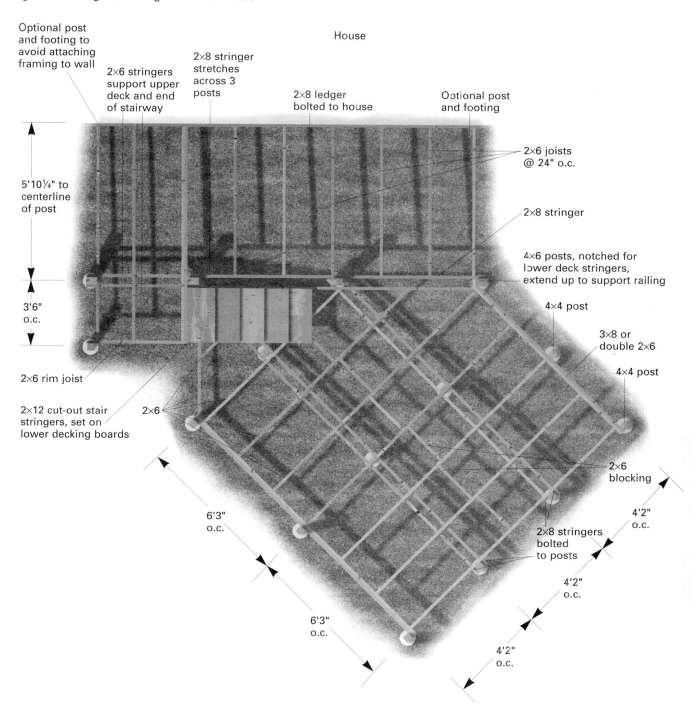

Optional post and footing to avoid attaching framing to wall

2×6 stringers support upper deck and end of stairway

2×8 stringer stretches across 3 posts

House

2×8 ledger bolted to house

Optional post and footing

2×6 joists @ 24" o.c.

5'10¼" to centerline of post

2×8 stringer

4×6 posts, notched for lower deck stringers, extend up to support railing

3'6" o.c.

4×4 post

3×8 or double 2×6

4×4 post

2×6 rim joist

2×12 cut-out stair stringers, set on lower decking boards

2×6

2×6 blocking

6'3" o.c.

4'2" o.c.

2×8 stringers bolted to posts

6'3" o.c.

4'2" o.c.

4'2" o.c.

A SPLIT-LEVEL DECK
continued

MATERIALS LIST

	Quantity	Material	Sizes
Footings	1.25 cu yd	concrete for 15 piers (8" dia. × 36") and 15 footings (18" dia. × 8")	
	15	metal post anchors	
	30	½"×4½" carriage bolts with nuts and washers	
Framing			
Posts	12	4×4s	Varies with site.
	3	4×6s	Varies with site.
Ledger		2×8	1 16'
Stringers	2	2×8s	8"
	6	2×8s	12'
	2	2×8s	14'
	2	2×8s	16'
	1	2×6	8'
Joists	9	2×6s	10'
	9	2×6s	12'
Blocking	2	2×6s	8'
Stair stringer	3	2×12s	8'
Joist hangers	29	2×6s	
	1	3×6	
	3	2×8s (for stair stringers)	
Ledger bolts	15	½"×5" lag screws with nuts and 75 washers	
Stringer bolts	34	½"×7" carriage bolts with nuts and washers	
Decking	50	2×6s	12'
Stair treads	4	2×6s	8' (cut into 4' lengths)
	2	2×2s	8' (cut into 4' lengths)
Railing and skirts			
Frame	22	2×4s	8'
	6	2×4s	10'
	5	2×4s	12'
	9	2×4s	14'
Sheathing and/or Siding		to cover 800 sq ft (568 on outside of deck, 216 on inside of railing + 2% waste)	
Moisture membrane	80 lineal feet	flashing	
Railing	6	2×6s	10'
	4	2×6s	12'
	4	2×6s	16'
Nails	5 lbs	joist hanger nails	
	15 lbs	16d HDG common nails	
	5 lbs	8d HDG common nails	
		Nails for sheathing/siding, depending on material used	
Screws	15 lbs	#8×3½" deck screws	

place. Where they attach to the 4×6 posts, you will have to cut notches so the stringers maintain the 3½-inch separation. This will provide strength and a flat surface to bolt to.

JOISTS: Attach hangers for the joists to the ledger and to the 2×8 stringer, and nail the joists in place with hangers. The joists that extend past the stairs have hangers only at one end. The rest of the support is provided by 2×6 stringers.

Hang the joists for the lower platform with joist hangers. Toenail them to the stringers as well. The short joists near the stairs have beveled ends, which you can mark by putting the joist in position and scribing a line along the bottom by tracing along the intersecting joist.

DECKING: Screw the decking in place. Because the interior posts were installed slightly long, you may need to trim two of them so they don't interfere with decking. Do so now, cutting the tops at about a 30-degree angle so they'll shed water. The third interior post will be a railing post for the stairs. Fit decking around it. Don't install the decking at the top of the stairs until you've fastened the stair stringers in place.

STAIRS: If the distance between deck surfaces is exactly 36 inches, the rise of each step will be 7³⁄₁₆ inches and the cut-out for the treads should be 11½ inches wide. The actual width of the treads will be 1½ inches wider to create an overhang. Cut out three 2×12 stringers. Attach them to the double 2×6 joist with joist hangers and toenail them to the decking at the bottom.

The topmost step is actually an extension of the upper decking. Install this decking, allowing the ends to run out over the stairway. Trim them once all the pieces are in place.

RAILINGS: The railing system for this deck is the same as that for the **Platform Deck with Steps** (see pages 64–69). Since this example has wood shingles, you would need to install ½-inch CDX plywood first. Then install the shingles, a sheet-metal cap, the 1×4 trim, and the 2×8 railing cap. The siding should be finished before treads are installed on the stairs.

FRAMING DETAIL

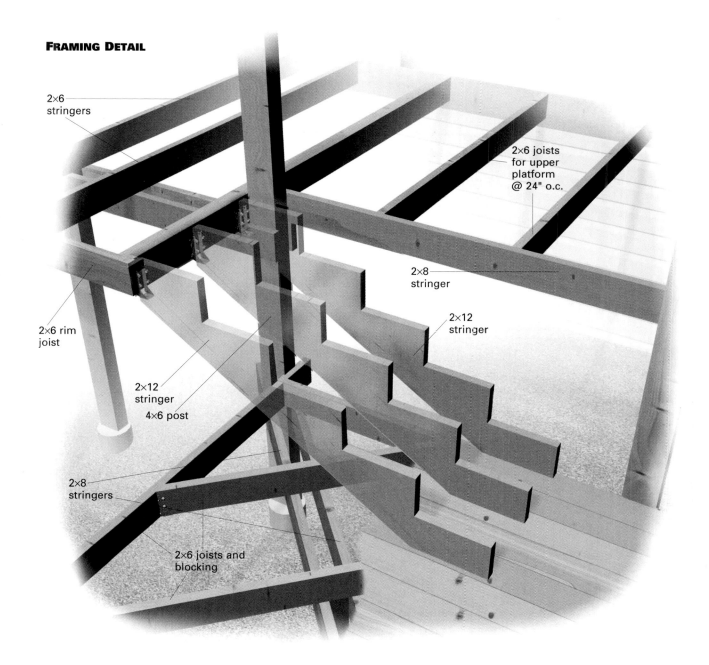

2×6 stringers

2×6 joists for upper platform @ 24" o.c.

2×6 rim joist

2×8 stringer

2×12 stringer

2×12 stringer

4×6 post

2×8 stringers

2×6 joists and blocking

DETAIL FOR CUTTING POST TOPS

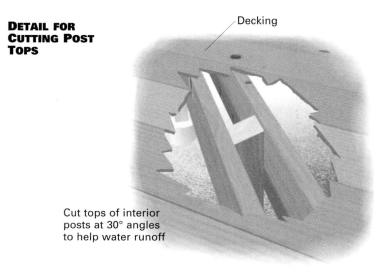

Decking

Cut tops of interior posts at 30° angles to help water runoff

A MULTILEVEL CASCADE

This seemingly complex and enormous deck is really a series of independent platforms, connected by stairways and steps. It is an ideal deck for a steeply-sloping site where the platforms can cascade downhill, providing an outdoor connection between a house's upper and lower floors.

This deck avoids a problem common to many high decks: It doesn't overshadow and darken the rooms below. The downstairs windows of this home still have sunlight and views because the parts of the deck are positioned away from the house.

The deck system consists of four platforms, two stairways of equal length, and an intermediate step between the two lower levels. Two of the platforms are attached to the house via ledgers and two are freestanding. The freestanding platforms and the outer edges of the attached platforms are supported by posts which bear on concrete piers. The piers extend into the ground to a point below the frost line.

The total height separation between the highest and lowest platforms depends on the distance between floor levels in the house—exactly 10 feet here. This overall distance determines the number and height of stair risers. These numbers will vary with site conditions and how steep you want the stairs to be (within code limitations). It is important that all stairs within the deck system have the same riser height.

PLAN VIEW INCLUDING POST LOCATION

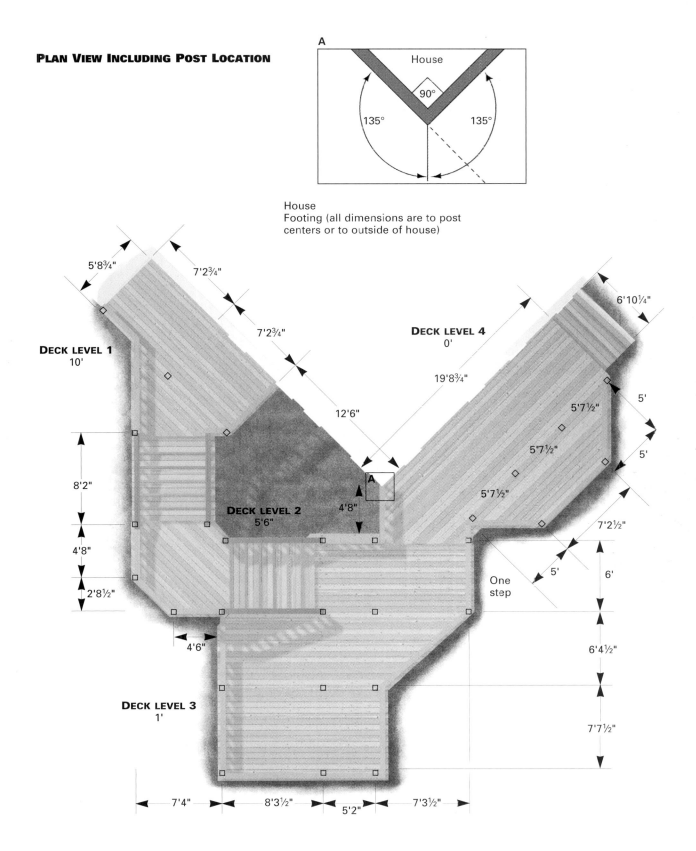

A

House

90°

135°   135°

House
Footing (all dimensions are to post
centers or to outside of house)

5'8¾"   7'2¾"

6'10¼"

7'2¾"

DECK LEVEL 4
0'

DECK LEVEL 1
10'

19'8¾"

5'7½"

5'

12'6"

5'7½"

5'

8'2"

DECK LEVEL 2
5'6"

5'7½"

4'8"

4'8"

5'7½"

7'2½"

2'8½"

One
step

5'

6'

4'6"

6'4½"

DECK LEVEL 3
1'

7'7½"

7'4"   8'3½"   7'3½"

5'2"

A MULTILEVEL CASCADE
continued

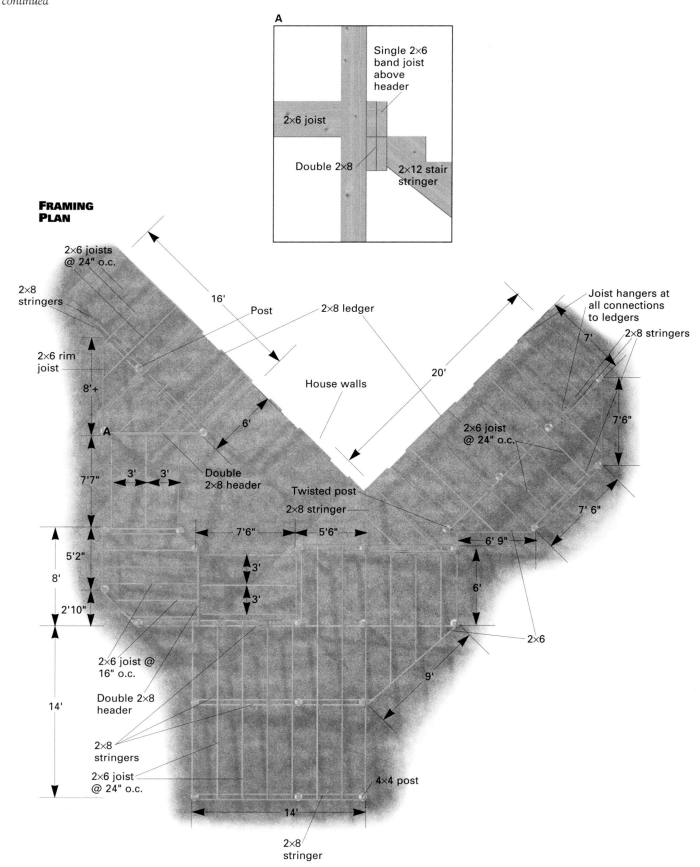

A

Single 2×6 band joist above header

2×6 joist

Double 2×8

2×12 stair stringer

FRAMING PLAN

2×6 joists @ 24" o.c.

2×8 stringers

2×6 rim joist

8'+

A

7'7"

3'   3'

Double 2×8 header

16'

Post

2×8 ledger

6'

House walls

20'

Twisted post

Joist hangers at all connections to ledgers

2×8 stringers

7'

7'6"

2×6 joist @ 24" o.c.

7' 6"

6' 9"

6'

5'2"

8'

2'10"

7'6"

5'6"

2×8 stringer

3'

3'

14'

2×6 joist @ 16" o.c.

Double 2×8 header

2×8 stringers

2×6 joist @ 24" o.c.

9'

2×6

4×4 post

14'

2×8 stringer

BUILDING THE DECK

This deck is not easy to build because of all the height variations and angles, especially if the site is sloped steeply. You can simplify construction by building the deck in sections. Build the platforms connected to the house first. Next, build the intermediate platforms, adjusting measurements to match the completed platforms. Building in stages is also a good approach if you are working with a tight budget.

LAYOUT AND FOOTINGS: Start by laying out the locations of the piers for the uppermost platform, using the dimensions given in the **Plan View and Post Layout** and the **Framing Plan**. Set batter boards and stretch a string parallel to the side of the house along the centers of the three main posts. Dig the holes for the footings and piers, set the forms, and pour the concrete. Set metal post anchors in the wet concrete.

Repeat the process for the lowest platform. Locate all the piers precisely because the posts that sit on top of them not only support the floor system they also act as railing posts.

LEDGERS AND POSTS: Bolt the 2×8 ledgers to the house, 2½ inches below the floor levels, following the procedures outlined on pages 62–63. Note that the ledger for the lower deck has a 2×8 stringer connected to it near the corner of the house. Be sure that the ledger is well bolted at that point. Bolt the posts to the piers, then plumb and brace them temporarily. Their heights will vary depending on the site. Do not cut them to exact length until you've built the deck platform.

STRINGERS AND JOISTS: Bolt the 2×8 stringers to the posts with two ⅜-inch bolts at each post. Position the top of the stringers 5½ inches below the top of the ledgers. In most cases, the stringers extend 1½ inch beyond the posts to carry the outermost joists. Hang double 2×8s at the top of each stairway. Attach the joists to the ledger with joist hangers. Their free ends are attached to a rim joist, which is bolted to the posts. Fasten the joists to the rim joist with joist hangers for maximum strength.

Where joists intersect rim joists at 45-degree angles, you can use 45-degree joist hangers, or face-nail three 16d nails through the rim joist into the main joist. The joists longer than 10 feet require blocking at their midpoint.

SECTION VIEW

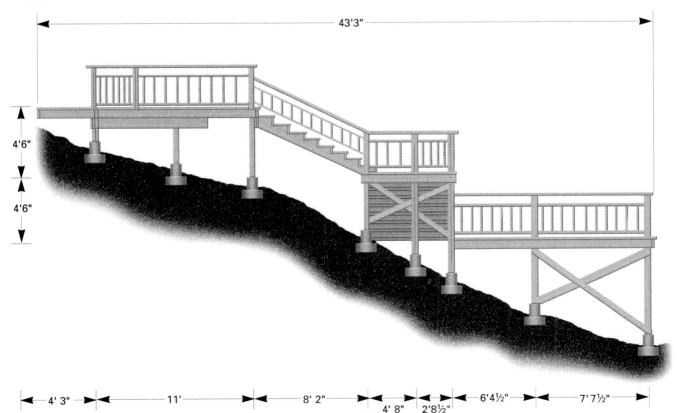

43'3"

4'6"

4'6"

4' 3"   11'   8' 2"   4' 8"   2'8½"   6'4½"   7'7½"

A MULTILEVEL CASCADE
continued

DECKING: Screw the 2×6 decking perpendicular to the joists on the three main platforms. On the small platform between the two stairways, the joists are 16 inches on center, so the decking can be installed diagonally to accentuate the deck's direction of flow. Allow the ends of the decking boards to overhang the band joists 3 or 4 inches.

STAIRS: Each stairway is supported by three 2×12 stringers. The actual dimensions and shape of the stringers vary with the overall rise and run of each stair. Calculate the shape of the stringers from the actual dimensions at the site itself, rather than the height on our plan. For more complete details on cutting stair stringers, see pages 28–31.

Attach the tops of the stringers to the double 2×8s with joist hangers. Attach the bottoms to the decking boards below with wood cleats. Nail the risers to the stringers, and then screw the treads in place. While the exact width of the treads will depend on the run of your stairway, you'll probably be able to use some combination of 2×6s and 2×2s as shown in the **Section Through Upper Platform**.

RAILINGS: The railings on this deck are supported by extensions of the 4×4 deck posts. Measure and cut each post so the top of the cap rail will be 36 inches above the decking (or as local codes require).

The easiest way to attach the horizontal rails is with metal framing clips shaped like pockets. Attach the clips to the posts first, and then slide the stringers into them. Once the stringers are in place, toenail 2×2 balusters between them. Spacing depends on local codes, but the usual requirement is for a maximum spacing of 4 inches. After the balusters are in place, nail the 2×6 cap rail to the top of the posts.

Because the distance between some of the posts is over 6 feet, the railing may tend to sag between them. To prevent this, cut a 2×4 block that will fit between the decking and the bottom rail at its midpoint and nail it in place. Do the same between the top rail and the cap rail.

MATERIALS LIST

	Quantity	Material	Sizes
Footings	2.8 cu yd	concrete for 28 piers (8" dia. × 36") and 28 footings (18" dia. × 8")	
	28	metal post anchors	
	56	½"×4½" carriage bolts with nuts and washers	
Framing			
Posts	4	4×4s	4' (approximate heights)
	6	4×4s	6'
	12	4×4s	8'
	6	4×4s	10'
Ledgers	2	2×8s	10'
	1	2×8	16'
Stringers	7	2×8s	8'
	2	2×8s	10'
	3	2×8s	12'
	5	2×8s	14'
	4	2×8s	16'
Band joists	7	2×6s	8'
	3	2×6s	10'
	2	2×6s	12'
	1	2×6	14'
	1	2×6	16'
Joists	10	2×6s	10'
	10	2×6s	12'
	8	2×6s	14'
	4	2×6s	16'
Blocking	6	2×6s	8'
Stair stringers	6	2×12s	10'
Joist hangers	20	2×6s	
	10	2×8s	
	1	45°	
Ledger bolts	60	½"×5" lag bolts and 360 washers	
Stringer bolts	30	⅜"×5½" with nuts and washers	
	28	⅜"×7" with nuts and washers	
	2	⅜"×9" with nuts and washers	
	2	⅜"×12" nuts and washers	
Decking and Stair Treads	1685 lineal feet	2×6s (700 sq ft of deck + 96 sq ft stairs + 2% waste)	
Railings			
Rails	12	2×4s	10'
	6	2×4s	12'
	6	2×4s	14'
	4	2×4s	16'
Balusters	260 lineal feet	2×2s (cut into 250 2' pieces + waste)	
Cap rail	1	2×6	8'
	5	2×6s	10'
	2	2×6s	12"
Nails	2 lbs	joist hanger nails	
	25 lbs	16d HDG common nails	
	10 lbs	8d HDG finish nails	
Screws	50 lbs	#8×3½" deck screws	

SECTION THROUGH UPPER PLATFORM

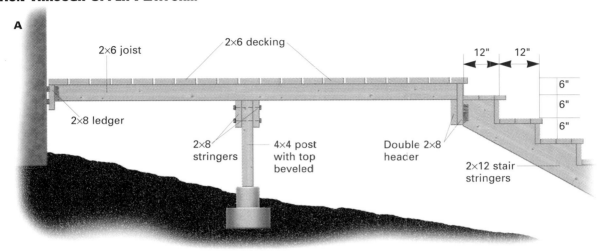

A
2×6 joist
2×6 decking
12" 12"
6"
6"
6"
2×8 ledger
2×8 stringers
4×4 post with top beveled
Double 2×8 header
2×12 stair stringers

SECTION THROUGH LOWER PLATFORM

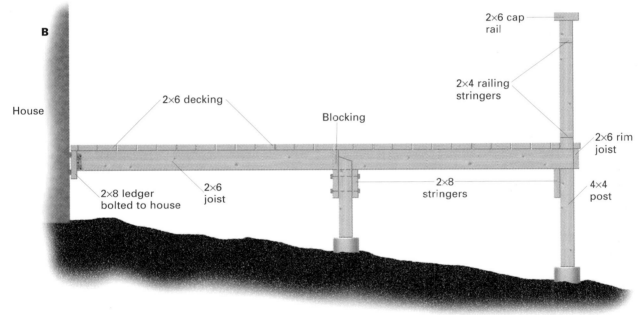

B
2×6 cap rail
House
2×6 decking
Blocking
2×4 railing stringers
2×6 rim joist
2×8 ledger bolted to house
2×6 joist
2×8 stringers
4×4 post

SECTION THROUGH MAIN PLATFORM

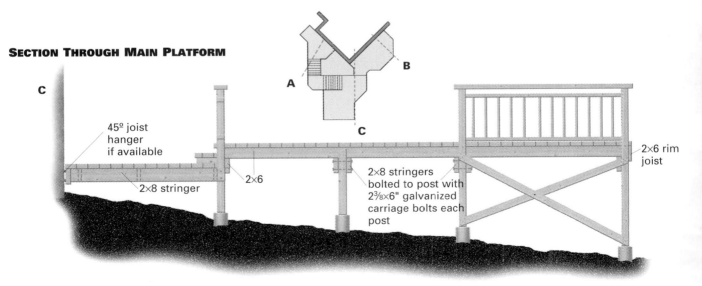

C
A
B
C
45º joist hanger if available
2×8 stringer
2×6
2×8 stringers bolted to post with 2³⁄₈×6" galvanized carriage bolts each post
2×6 rim joist

A DECK AND STORAGE COMBINATION

If your site requires a tall deck and you wonder what to do with the space underneath, consider enclosing it for storage. This deck was designed for access from the second floor with a good-sized storage bay below. A large doorway provides easy access, while two end windows allow cross ventilation.

The key to this plan is a durable roofing material that is suitable for flat roofs and does not require frequent maintenance or renewal. A variety of such materials allows you to install a permanent wood deck over them. Most of them are rubberlike substances that you paint onto the roof. Some are solid membranes that you roll out. Both types are superior to ordinary roll roofing or tar and gravel, but much more expensive. Even if you

do not need (or can't afford) an enclosed space beneath your new deck right now, consider including the roofing. It will create a sheltered area that you could either leave open or enclose and finish at a later time.

To find out which roofing products work best in your area, consult a local roofing supplier, sealant specialist, or professional roofing company. You will probably find that some of the materials can withstand direct traffic, but it is advisable to cover them with boards to prolong their life. For all the advantages of this type of roofing, the one main disadvantage is the difficulty of locating leaks. The usual remedy is to recoat the entire surface.

The framing for this deck is essentially the same as that which you would build for an addition. A 2×4 stud wall set on a continuous foundation supports the roof, which is framed with 2×10 joists, 16 inches on center. In fact, structural grade 2×8s would be enough for the 12-foot span, but because the framing must carry a roof and possibly a finished ceiling in addition to the deck itself, it is better to use 2×10s.

The roof is sheathed with plywood (which works perfectly with the 12-by-16-foot dimensions). It is covered with a waterproof membrane. Sleepers are laid in place and the decking is fastened down. Railings and a gutter system add the finishing touches.

CONSIDERATIONS BEFORE BUILDING

This deck is designed as an addition to a split-level home. Not all sites will be the same, but there are some common design issues you must consider before using this plan.

First, what impact will this deck have on downstairs rooms? Will you have to close off windows or add a doorway? Will the deck make the downstairs too dark?

Second, how will you use the space under the deck? If you are not enclosing it with walls, then you can support the deck with a post-and-beam system similar to that used for other decks in this book. If you wish to use the enclosure for living space, then you must make sure the slab is moisture-proof,. You'll need insulation and heating, access to the house, and utility lines in your plans.

BUILDING THE DECK

FOUNDATION: Unlike most other decks, this design requires a continuous perimeter foundation to keep the walls above grade and to provide adequate support for the entire structure. If the lower floor will be concrete, codes usually require a 6-inch foundation wall on a 12-inch-wide footing. If you want the lower floor to be a wood floor on a joist system, then your foundation must support two floors. This usually requires an 8-inch foundation wall on a 15-inch-wide footing.

Set batter boards and stretch strings out from the house to locate the corners of the structure. Dig 2-foot-wide trenches below frost level for the footings. Drill three holes into the house foundation where the new foundation will meet it, and insert short (30") pieces of rebar to tie the new to the old. Build forms for the footings with 2×8s, making sure they are level and rigidly staked. Some codes require that the footing and foundation be poured at the same time. If so, build the forms

for the foundation wall, and place the concrete. Other codes require a separate pour for each part, with the foundation fitting into a recess in the footing. If separate pours are required, pour the footing; while the concrete is still wet, sink a 2×4 into the surface to form a recess. Remove the 2×4 well before the concrete dries. After the footings set, build forms for the foundation, and snap a level line inside the forms to mark the top of the foundation. Brace the forms well. Pour concrete into the recess and fill the forms. Sink anchor bolts for the walls in the wet concrete a minimum of every 4 feet.

PLAN VIEW OF DECKING

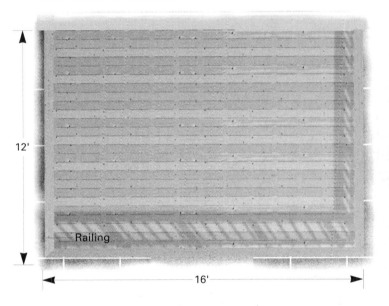

12'

Railing

16'

PLAN VIEW OF ROOM BELOW

5'　6'　5'

House wall

4×3 foot window

4×3 foot window

4'

4'

4'

Foundation footing

Foundation wall

2×4 stud wall

Two 3'×6'8" doors

A DECK AND STORAGE COMBINATION
continued

LEDGER AND WALL FRAMING: The bolting detail for this ledger is different from other decks. Because it will be protected from the weather, there is no need to leave a gap between the ledger and wall. Instead, strip away the siding, and bolt the ledger to the framing 5 inches below floor level.

Build the outside wall next. It should end a foot below the top of the ledger to account for floor joists and a ¼-inch-per-foot slope for drainage. Begin the wall by bolting a pressure-treated sill to the foundation. Calculate the height of the wall and cut the studs to length. Nail together the wall and tip it into position, bracing it to keep it plumb and square. Frame the rest of the walls the same way.

JOISTS: Because the joists slope away from the house, you need to cut their ends at a slight angle so they meet the ledger properly and so that the rim joist will be plumb. Hang the joists from the ledger with joist hangers. Before nailing the joists in place, cut a small notch in their undersides to fit the joist

hangers, again to accommodate the slope. The other end will not rest flat on the wall plates, so you must bevel it as well.

Nail the rim joist to the ends of the joists, and install blocking as shown. The top edge of the rim joist may have to be beveled to make it flush with the tops of the joists. Attach the joists to the wall's top sill with seismic anchors. Even if they're not required by local code, they make attaching the joists much easier.

WALL AND ROOF SHEATHING: Install the wall sheathing or plywood siding first so the roof sheathing will overlap it. Lay tongue-and-groove plywood roof sheathing across the joints. Cut the sheets in half, as needed, to stagger the end joints and trim the sheets so the outside edges are flush with the siding.

ROOFING MEMBRANE: Prepare the plywood roof sheathing for the type of roofing material you plan to use. Usually this means caulking all the seams, priming the plywood with a special paint compatible with the membrane, and nailing a drip edge around the edges. Apply the roofing material according to the manufacturer's recommendations.

FOUNDATION OPTIONS

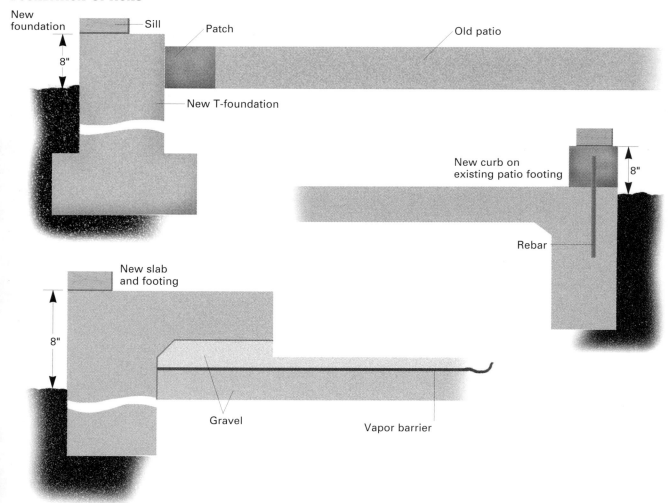

SLEEPERS AND DECKING: After the roofing membrane is thoroughly dry, install angle flashing against the house, prying siding boards loose so it can be tucked up under the house siding. Nail 2×4 sleepers above all the joists. To keep water from following the nails down through the roof membrane, caulk the bottom of each sleeper where the nails will penetrate it before setting it in place. Also caulk the nail heads after setting them. You also may want to level the deck by putting shims under the sleepers every 16 inches.

Screw the decking boards into the sleepers with #8×2½-inch screws so they do not penetrate through the sleepers into the roofing; otherwise, the roof will leak. Install the decking to overhang the roof by ¼ to ⅜ inch.

SECTION VIEW

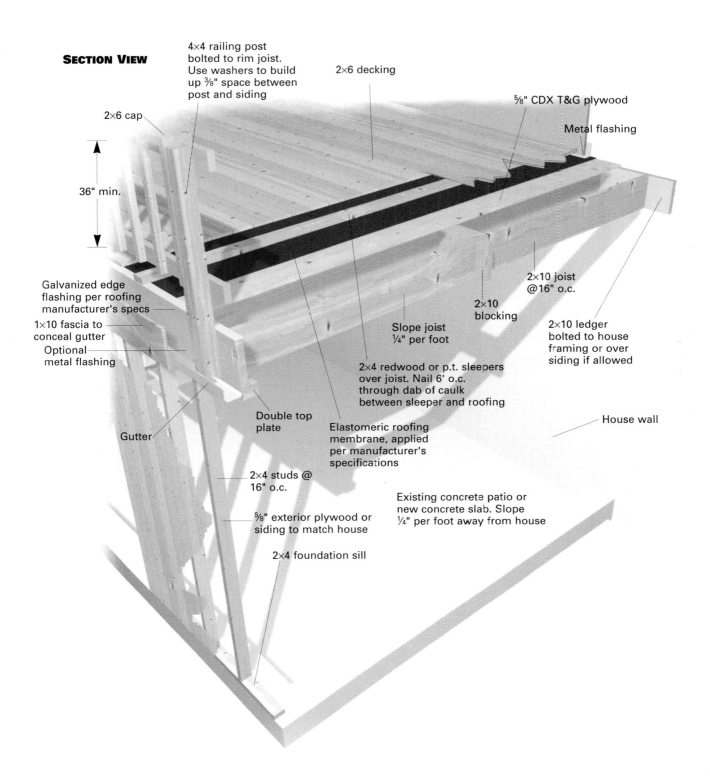

- 4×4 railing post bolted to rim joist. Use washers to build up ⅜" space between post and siding
- 2×6 decking
- ⅝" CDX T&G plywood
- Metal flashing
- 2×6 cap
- 36" min.
- Galvanized edge flashing per roofing manufacturer's specs
- 1×10 fascia to conceal gutter
- Optional metal flashing
- Gutter
- Double top plate
- Slope joist ¼" per foot
- 2×10 blocking
- 2×10 joist @16" o.c.
- 2×10 ledger bolted to house framing or over siding if allowed
- 2×4 redwood or p.t. sleepers over joist. Nail 6' o.c. through dab of caulk between sleeper and roofing
- Elastomeric roofing membrane, applied per manufacturer's specifications
- House wall
- 2×4 studs @ 16" o.c.
- ⅝" exterior plywood or siding to match house
- 2×4 foundation sill
- Existing concrete patio or new concrete slab. Slope ¼" per foot away from house

A DECK AND STORAGE COMBINATION
continued

GUTTER AND DOWNSPOUT:
Hang the gutter about 8 inches down from the roof surface, sloped about 1/8-inch-per-foot to help it drain. To prevent water slipping behind the gutter, slide long, straight flashing up under the edge of the roof flashing, and let its lower edge lap the gutter. Attach a downspout to the low end of the gutter and mount it to the siding.

RAILING: This deck has an open railing in order to preserve as much of the view as possible. Bolt the posts through the flashing and siding to the rim joist with 3/8-inch by 7-inch carriage bolts. Slip a stack of five washers on the bolts between the post and the flashing/siding to allow for air circulation. For added protection from water, caulk the holes before you slide the bolts through

After the posts are installed, nail the top and bottom 2×4s in place. Nail 2×2 balusters between the 2×4s, spacing them so the openings do not exceed local code requirements (4 inches maximum, typically). Nail on a 2×6 cap rail, mitering the corners. If you want to conceal the gutter, nail a 1×12 fascia board to the outside of the railing posts so that it drops to cover the gutter.

FINISHING THE ENCLOSED SPACE: Install the doors using jambs, threshold, and casings that match the existing house. Trim the windows, corners, and any other features of the enclosure to match.

MATERIALS LIST

	Quantity	Material	Sizes
Foundation (40 lineal feet of perimeter foundation)			
	2.6 cu yd	concrete (for 6"×30" wall and 6"×12" footing)	
	140 feet	#4 rebar	
	1 roll	tie wire	
	10	1/2"×10" anchor bolts with nuts and washers	
Shed Framing			
Ledger	1	2×10	16'
Sill (pressure-treated)			
	1	2×4	10'
	2	2×4s	12'
Studs	46	2×4s	8'
Plates	4	2×4s	12'
	2	2×4s	16'
Headers	2	2×6s	8'
	2	2×6s	10'
Joists	13	2×10s	12'
	1	2×10	16'
Blocking	2	2×10s	8'
Joist hangers	13	2×10s	
Shims	1 bundle		
Sheathing/Siding			
Roof	6	4×8s	1/2" T&G exterior plywood
Walls	9	4×9s	5/8" exterior plywood
Exterior Finish			
Roofing	40'	galvanized edge flashing	
	16'	3"×3" galvanized angle flashing	
	192 sq ft	roofing material	
Windows	2	4'×3' prehung units to match existing house	
Doors	2	3'×6'8" exterior doors, and jambs and hardware	
Trim	90 lineal feet	for corners, windows, and door (to match existing house)	
Deck			
Sleepers	13	2×4s	12'
Decking	24	2×6s	16'
Railing			
Posts	13	4×4s	4'
Rails	4	2×4s	12'
	2	2×4s	16'
Balusters	27	2×2s	8' lengths (cut into 80 30" pieces)
Cap Rails	2	2×6s	12'
	1	2×6s	16'
Fascia	1	1×12	16'
Bolts	26	3/8"×7" carriage bolts with nuts and 156 washers (spacers)	
Gutter	16' and hangers and downspout		
Nails	2 lbs	joist hanger nails	
	10 lbs	12d HDG common nails	
	10 lbs	16d HDG common nails	
Screws	12 lbs	#8×2 1/2" deck screws	
Caulking	6 tubes	sealant for roof sheathing seams, trim pieces, windows, and sleepers	

DECK, ROOF, AND FRAMING PLAN

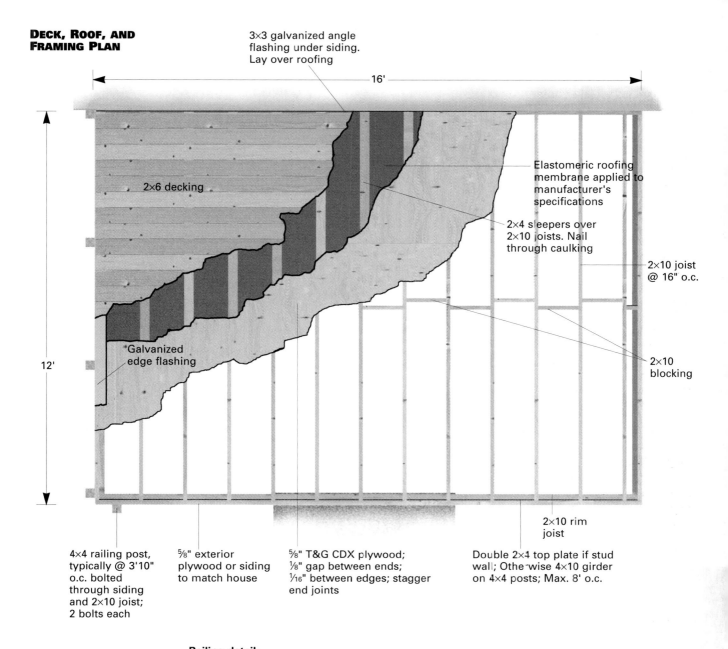

3×3 galvanized angle flashing under siding. Lay over roofing

16'

2×6 decking

Galvanized edge flashing

12'

Elastomeric roofing membrane applied to manufacturer's specifications

2×4 sleepers over 2×10 joists. Nail through caulking

2×10 joist @ 16" o.c.

2×10 blocking

2×10 rim joist

4×4 railing post, typically @ 3'10" o.c. bolted through siding and 2×10 joist; 2 bolts each

⅝" exterior plywood or siding to match house

⅝" T&G CDX plywood; ⅛" gap between ends; 1/16" between edges; stagger end joints

Double 2×4 top plate if stud wall; Otherwise 4×10 girder on 4×4 posts; Max. 8' o.c.

Railing detail; varies with style

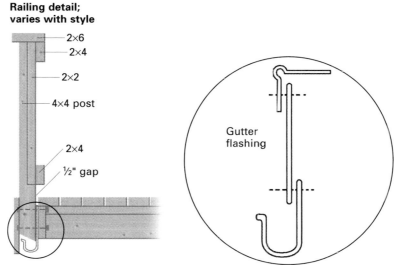

2×6
2×4
2×2
4×4 post
2×4
½" gap

Gutter flashing

GLOSSARY

Anchor. Metal device embedded in wet concrete for attaching posts to piers.

Baluster. Vertical railing member, held between top and bottom rails.

Band joist. Joist attached to the ends of field joists. Sometimes refers to any joist on the perimeter of the deck. Also called rim joist.

Beam. Major structural member. The thick horizontal timber that rests on top of posts and in turn supports joists or decking. Can be solid or built up of 2 or more 2-bys. Also called a girder.

Blocking. Short pieces of lumber cut from joist material and nailed perpendicularly between joists to stabilize them.

Bracing. Diagonal crosspieces nailed and bolted between tall posts, usually those over 5 feet tall.

Cantilever. The end portion of a joist, or of the entire deck, that extends out beyond the beam.

Durable species. Wood species that are naturally resistant to decay and insect damage, such as heart redwood, heart cedar, tidewater cypress, and some locusts. Sometimes refers to other woods that have been pressure-treated.

Earth-wood clearance. The minimum distance required between the ground and any wood. The exception is pressure-treated or durable species lumber specified for ground contact.

Elevation. Drawing of a proposed structure as it looks from the side.

Fascia. Nonstructural, horizontal trim piece that covers the ends of deck boards and part or all of the band joist.

Flashing. Aluminum, copper, or galvanized sheet metal used to cover joints where moisture might enter a structure.

Footing. The bottom portion of any foundation or pier; it distributes weight to the ground. For decks, it often refers to the concrete structure consisting of the pier as well as its footing.

Frost line. The lowest depth at which the ground will freeze. It determines the code-required depth for footings.

Grade. The top surface of the ground. Grading also refers to the act of excavating, leveling, and compacting dirt to its desired finished level.

Hot-dipped galvanized (HDG) nails. Nails dipped in zinc rather than electroplated. Superior for outdoor construction.

Joist. 2-by lumber, set on edge, that supports decking. It is supported by beams, ledgers, stringers, or header joists.

Joist hanger. Metal connecting device for attaching a joist at right angles to a ledger or header joist so their top edges are flush.

KDAT (Kiln Dried After Treatment). Pressure-treated lumber that has been dried after being treated with preservative. It is more expensive than regular pressure-treated lumber (which isn't dried) but much less likely to warp.

Lag screw or bolt. Heavy-duty screw with a bolt head for attaching structural members to a wall or to material too thick for a machine bolt to go through.

Ledger. A 2-by or wider piece of lumber bolted to the house for supporting the ends of joists. Technically refers only to a board placed under the joist ends, but often refers to any member bolted to the house.

Loads. The weights and forces any structure is designed to counteract, such as dead load (the structure itself), live loads (all potential occupants and furnishings, snow load, wind uplift, and earthquake forces).

Pier. A small concrete or masonry structure that holds a post off the ground. It has its own footing and can be precast or cast in place.

Plumb. Perfectly vertical.

Pressure treatment. A process of forcing preservatives into wood. One commonly used waterborne preservative is chromated copper arsenate (CCA), specified for aboveground (LP-2) or ground-contact (LP-22) use. Depending on the chemical used, the wood will have a greenish or brownish tint.

Reinforcing bar. Steel rods for reinforcing concrete, sometimes called rebar or rerod.

Riser. In stair construction, the vertical dimension or "rise" of any step.

Screening. The maximum opening allowed between railing members. The distance varies by code (often 4 inch maximum).

Sleeper. A horizontal wood member laid directly on ground, patio, or roof for supporting a deck.

Slope. Ground with an inclined surface, usually measured as a percentage (units of vertical rise per 100 units of horizontal distance).

Span. The distance between supports, measured center to center.

Spindle. Small-dimensioned baluster.

Stair stringers. The heavy, inclined members that support a stairway's treads. Can be solid, with treads attached between the stringers, or cut out, with treads resting on top of the sawtooth sections. Also called carriages.

Zoning requirements. Local ordinances that may affect a deck's size or location, such as setback limits (minimum distance from the property line to the structure), lot coverage (maximum percentage of the lot that can be covered by all improvements), and even the deck's size or height.

INDEX

Boldface numbers indicate pages with photographs or illustrations related to the topic.

METRIC CONVERSIONS

U.S. Units to Metric Equivalents			Metric Units to U.S. Equivalents		
To Convert From	Multiply By	To Get	To Convert From	Multiply By	To Get
Inches	25.4	Millimetres	Millimetres	0.0394	Inches
Inches	2.54	Centimetres	Centimetres	0.3937	Inches
Feet	30.48	Centimetres	Centimetres	0.0328	Feet
Feet	0.3048	Metres	Metres	3.2808	Feet
Yards	0.9144	Metres	Metres	1.0936	Yards
Square inches	6.4516	Square centimetres	Square centimetres	0.1550	Square inches
Square feet	0.0929	Square metres	Square metres	10.764	Square feet
Square yards	0.8361	Square metres	Square metres	1.1960	Square yards
Cubic inches	16.387	Cubic centimetres	Cubic centimetres	0.0610	Cubic inches
Cubic feet	0.0283	Cubic metres	Cubic metres	35.315	Cubic feet
Cubic feet	28.316	Litres	Litres	0.0353	Cubic feet
Cubic yards	0.7646	Cubic metres	Cubic metres	1.308	Cubic yards
Cubic yards	764.55	Litres	Litres	0.0013	Cubic yards

To convert from degrees Fahrenheit (F) to degrees Celsius (C), first subtract 32, then multiply by $\frac{5}{9}$.

To convert from degrees Celsius to degrees Fahrenheit, multiply by $\frac{9}{5}$, then add 32.